FUNNY MUMMY

JENNY WYNTER

Published by Share Your Story Publishing
and Funny Mummies 2019

Second Edition 2022

Copyright © 2019 Jenny Wynter
www.jennywynter.com

All rights reserved. No part of this publication may be reproduced, stored in a retrieval system, or transmitted in any form or by any means, electronic, mechanical, photocopying, recording or otherwise, without the prior written permission from the publisher.

Disclaimer

Every effort has been made to ensure that this book is free from error or omissions. Information provided is of general nature only and should not be considered legal or financial advice. The intent is to offer a variety of information to the reader. However, the author, publisher, editor or their agents or representatives shall not accept responsibility for any loss or inconvenience caused to a person or organisation relying on this information.

A catalogue record for this book is available from the National Library of Australia.

Book cover design and formatting services by Self-publishingLab.com

ISBN:

978-0-6482270-8-3 (pbk)
978-0-6482270-9-0 (e-bk)

Contents

Chapter 1	That's My Mum Onstage	1
Chapter 2	It Takes a Retirement Village	21
Chapter 3	When Following Your Dreams Is So Exciting Your Period Stops	39
Chapter 4	I'm Being A Vagina And They Hate Me	53
Chapter 5	You Know, If You Wanna Stay in Canada Forever, It's Real Easy…	67
Chapter 6	Car Crashes And Caboolture	93
Chapter 7	The Year My Life Broke	119
Chapter 8	Life In The Departure Lounge	139
Chapter 9	Sometimes You Just Need A Nap	149
Chapter 10	The Life Changing Magic Of ~~Tidying~~ Hooking Up	153
Chapter 11	Episode IV: A New Hope	159
Chapter 12	What It's Like To Be A Mother In Comedy	167
Chapter 13	Funny Mummies	171
Chapter 14	The Best Free Advice You Will Ever Get	181
Bonus Content		189

FUNNY MUMMY

Smile, though your heart is aching
Smile, even though it's breaking
When there are clouds in the sky you'll get by

If you smile through your fear and sorrow
Smile and maybe tomorrow,
You'll see the sun come shining through
for you

Light up your face with gladness
Hide every trace of sadness
Although a tear may be ever so near
That's the time you must keep on trying

Smile what's the use of crying
You'll find that life is still worthwhile
If you'll just Smile

Lyrics by John Turner and Geoffrey Parsons

Acknowledgements

It takes a village to raise a child, a retirement village to raise me and a creative village to raise a book!

Special shout outs to my team of champions who helped make this book happen by reading, re-reading, editing, suggesting and doing it all with so much encouragement and kindness and all-round rockstar-edness: Michelle Worthington, Elaine Denning, Helen Goodwin and my hubby Jon.

Also I must say MEGA props to my beloved community of Funny Mummies. You lot are hilarious and delightful and I bloody love what we've created. And to anybody who's ever come out to see a Funny Mummies Comedy Gala show, thank you, thank you, thank you. You deserve all the lollipops and massages.

And finally, thank you to my family, to my mothers - both of you - and to my kidlets for your infinite inspiration. The royalty cheque's in the mail[*].

Jen xxx

---

[*] Mail: like email you can hold in your hands.

Preface

'Make people laugh.'

While this might sound like something you'd read on a boho cushion from Kmart, this was in fact, one of the last things said by my grandmother – who, for reasons you'll understand as you read on, I called my Mum – to me just before she died. For as long as I can remember, she'd been telling my sister and me that when life smacked you squarely in the guts, the one thing you could control was whether you were going to laugh or cry. 'And I know which one I'd prefer!' she'd say.

I hasten to add that in spite of her steadfast philosophy, she certainly did do her fair share of crying. As do I. Her life advice was not to 'turn it off like a light switch' *Book of Mormon* style, but rather to force yourself to find the funny in it. Even if you can't right away, keep trying. Because it's usually there. Sometimes the funny is so dark you'd never dare even share it with anyone else, but then humour, while wonderful, is not always meant to be light.

Whether light or dark though, what it *is* about, is relief.

From stress, from awfulness, from reality…

Laughter, I'm convinced, is life's epidural. Or rather, life's gas mask. It doesn't entirely negate the sensations of pain; you still feel them, but even for a few intakes of breath, you can forget: the edge is taken off and you believe that, in spite of everything, yes you can still feel joy and light and you might just make it through.

These days, we need comedy more than ever. It's how the poor have dealt with the injustices of the powerful since the beginning of time: by making fun of them. Cartoonists make light of even heavy political problems. We see reflections of ourselves on screen to poke fun at; sometimes as it's just easier than to poke fun at ourselves. I have wondered at times whether pursuing a career in comedy is just self-indulgent bullshit, but I firmly believe that it's not a luxury, it's a necessity.

In my work as a Clown Doctor – where for several years I have performed in hospital wards and rooms to provide comic relief and distraction for patients and their families – the examples of this I've experienced are extreme. While on the surface it might seem like we're just there to provide 5-10 minutes of light entertainment, the reality is that often the effect remains long after we've left the room. Humour is a mood changer. So often we walk out of a hospital room and can hear the family continuing to talk and chuckle about what just happened.

A history of trauma, sadness or mental illness seems to be a pretty common thread between almost all comedians, so much so that those without it almost deserve their own label: 'Certified Trauma-Free!' So, when it comes to my own sadness/comedy combo, I'm not a unique little snowflake. But I do hope that in sharing my own story, it might be a call to arms for you to proactively find, create and embrace the funny into your life.

It's NOT a luxury.

It's NOT a selfish pursuit.

Funny Mummy

It's vital: you must secure your own nitrous oxide mask first.

> *Life is an unexpected variety show*
> *It's full of mind-blowing highs,*
> *It's full of soul-crushing lows.*
> *There're happy bits, and crappy bits,*
> *Some parts just give you the shits.*
> *There's twists and turns and bends,*
> *There's parts that you wish would just end, when you're singing*
> *'Things did not turn out the way I wanted…'*

— From my cabaret *An Unexpected Variety Show*

Chapter 1 That's My Mum Onstage

I have no idea that the smell of cigarettes and beer aren't familiar to every four-year-old. Nor do I think 'that's my Mummy on the stage!' is in any way a remarkable thought.

But many of my earliest memories are set in pubs. Ironically, those memories are just as fuzzy as my later ones would be, though for different reasons. My Mum, a gorgeous Scandinavian looking woman with long wavy blonde hair and big blue eyes, is a singer/songwriter, and as a single mum, her simple solution to not having easy access to child-minding is to take her two very young children, my younger sister Ang and me, along to her gigs. I feel equal parts proud and jealous. Not jealous of the attention she's getting from the audience, but rather the attention that she's giving TO the audience. They seem enamoured with her, but they can't be. Not more than me.

She is stunningly beautiful. Admittedly, I'm highly biased, though judging by her shockingly large number of male admirers, I'm not the only one who thinks so. Even as an adult, if I had a dollar for the number of men who've told me with no shame whatsoever that they were completely in love with her… Well, I'd never need to purchase a supermarket trolley token again.

Unfortunately, one of these men is Tom.

Tom is not my Dad. He's not my little sister's Dad either.

My actual Dad had a whirlwind love affair with my Mum, which was deemed so scandalous – him being a whopping 24 years older, making her younger than a couple of his own children – that my grandmother apparently threatened to shoot him. They shot through to northern Queensland where she was loved up, then knocked up, then gave up on the relationship and returned back to

Chapter 1 That's My Mum Onstage

Toowoomba with her tail between the legs from which I would soon emerge.

I will meet him when I'm three, and I will spend the odd weekend visiting him on his farm, with his new Filipino wife Patricia and my little brother Billy, whom I adore.

Ang's Dad likewise had a scandalous love affair – in this case, an actual marital affair – with our Mum, and by all reports for possibly the first time in her colourful relationship history, she was the one who had her heart broken. Which, many years later when Ang finally tracks him down, makes complete sense. He is funny, musical, country, charismatic: everything I would ever imagine the mother I have in my mind loving.

Prior to my and then Ang's arrival, was that of our big brother Jamie. At 23, our mum actually marries his Dad in the first and only wedding she'd ever have. This partnership lasts long enough for Jamie to reach early childhood and for them to decide that he is better off living with his father.

Jamie comes and visits us some weekends and school holidays, and I think he is the most wonderful human in the world. He makes me laugh constantly, like some kind of personal, one-on-one clown, and when it's time for him to leave I cry and cry and cry.

Three children. Three different dads. Our grandmother is appalled. Years later somebody will tell me that my mum once said 'My Mum's always so ashamed of me when I get pregnant. But God, she loves the babies!'

In spite of all the men in her life, for the bulk of my childhood my only experience of a man in the household is Tom. Tom has a big red bushy beard and plays the flute in a duo with my Mum which has been quick to gain some traction playing gigs around South East Queensland.

He is quick to anger and hits us both. One day he throws a hot water bottle at my face while I'm eating an ice-block; the ice-block splits my lip.

He's an arsehole.

I hate him.

He's terrifying – one day I hear him ask Mum if she's going to marry him – I nearly vomit.

Years later, I still struggle with the question of why the hell she didn't leave him. It was one thing to stay in a

Chapter 1   That's My Mum Onstage

relationship with somebody who's hurting you, but your kids too? How could she do that to us? I was angry. Many years later my uncle explains to me that she *was* trying to leave him. But he just wouldn't leave her house. He plainly refused to leave. How the hell do you make somebody go if they just won't?

Knowing this information makes a huge difference to me. She didn't just willingly accept someone hurting her children. She wanted to do something about it. But like so many women in these kinds of situations she found that wanting something and having it actually happen are two very different things. People tend to judge these women just as I judged my own mother, but they underestimate how incredibly difficult it can be to actually get out even if you want to.

But, that dark part of our lives aside, my childhood is still pretty happy. My mum is creative and engaged with us: we bake cookies, we ride bikes, we go to the beach and we practise my jazz ballet routines in the front yard. I LOVE ballet. I'm practising like crazy in preparation for our end of semester performance of *Alice In Wonderland*, where I play... da da da DA... a piggy! (Was there a piggy in actual *Alice In Wonderland*? I don't think there was, but what the hell does that matter, THERE IS NOW!) My mum and I go to the dancewear shop and check out the little outfit I'm

supposed to wear. It's basically a black leotard covered in dark pink sequins and I am utterly, utterly in love with it! I keep nagging Mum to make sure we get the suit in time. She hushes me and promises we will soon. There is plenty of time. There is plenty of time.
There is plenty of time.

She is a truly beautiful parent… when she's there.

I am left to my own devices far more than I should be. As a result, I'm exposed to some incredibly inappropriate film and television by the tender age of four. I can still see a disturbing scene of a policeman hopping in a hot tub with two topless ladies who then proceed to tear his body apart because da da daaaaaa… they are vampires. I see boobs upon boobs upon boobs. And possibly the most disturbing of all, is a movie called *Lipstick*, about a model who is repeatedly tied up and raped by a photographer. At the end – spoiler warning – when she finds out he's also been making the moves on her kid sister; she grabs a gun and shoots him dead.

I cannot stress this enough: I AM UNDER FIVE. I have no idea what the real lasting impact of this crazy early exposure to watching the world of sex – or movie sex, at

Chapter 1 That's My Mum Onstage

least – was; it's not like sexual abuse in that I wasn't exploited by somebody with power over me, but there was certainly a loss of innocence somewhere along the line.

In spite of some evidence to the contrary, I do still consider my Mum to be a good Mum.

I get it.

As a parent… let alone a single one… let alone a single one with dreams… you sometimes let the kids do their own thing just so you can have a break. Sometimes 'their own thing' just goes on a little longer than planned, or than is necessarily healthy. I don't want you to get the impression that I lived in a house full of movies about sexual abuse and violence. I mean, yes, I saw way more than my fair share of stuff that was beyond questionable but interspersed with this was also the good stuff – the more appropriate stuff.

The Muppet Movie. Mary Poppins. And my absolute lifetime favourite, Franco Zeffirelli's *Romeo and Juliet.*

All of these Mum had taped off the telly; I still remember Tybalt slaying Mercutio followed immediately by a Dreamworld ad. And if my 'seeing things WAY beyond my age' had resulted in anything positive, it was that somehow this kindergartener became absolutely besotted with the classic Shakespearean tale. The costumes, the actors (still to this day two of the most utterly stunning humans the world has ever seen on-screen) and the music. All of it. It killed me. But then, what was this? At the end, after all the fighting, the kissing and the longing… THEY. KILL. THEMSELVES!

I am utterly bereft. I sob and sob and sob until I have nothing left, which is as long as it takes the video cassette to rewind and I immediately start it all over again.

It is my first contact with death.

Not a goldfish, not a great grandmother, but a fictional pair of star-crossed lovers speaking words I can barely understand yet somehow, I do understand: that death is final.

That it is devastating.

And that it is irrevocable.

My mum is like night and day – or day and night, as it were. Day times, she is very hands on. She takes us for bike rides, me on the yellow joy machine I'd been over the moon to get

Chapter 1   That's My Mum Onstage

for my birthday, she with her green machine with Angie perching happily on the back. I'm her 'little Jenny Wren!' or 'Wren' for short. We spend hours playing in the surf, we bake cookies, we juice and make smoothies, we read, we draw, we sing: it is daytime, and she is my sun.

Then, night comes, and she disappears.

Either literally, going out to gigs, or metaphorically, making herself as small as possible to avoid Tom's rage-fuelled outbursts.

Either way, I miss her. I miss the daytime. I miss the warmth. I miss the light.

Sometimes when she is out performing, she leaves my sister and me overnight at a babysitter's house. I remember one night being so upset by her departure, that the only way she can comfort me is by promising that she will be back before I wake up. I am comforted, namely because in my little head I'd decided that I was not even going to sleep. I will stay up as late as I have to, ready to surprise her and leap straight back into her arms. I lay in my bed and stare out at the road, where a single lonely streetlight illuminates not much more than the gutter. I am quiet and still and not at all tired. I lie there and wait. And wait. And wait. The sun comes up and the streetlight goes out. Still nothing. Has something terrible – of Shakespearean proportions – happened? Deep down I know it hasn't. She just hasn't come to get us. But it still hurts.

Decades later I will find myself playing out this pattern with my own kids, as I become a performer having to leave them behind as I go out at night to do gigs. I will wonder whether it's hurting them but tell myself that I am fully within my rights to pursue my own passions. I will realise the never-ending pull between my creative dreams and my children and be constantly questioning whether I am serving either properly. But I'm getting ahead of myself…

I'm five years old. I'm drinking a glass of milk and as I go to put it on the kitchen bench, somehow, I miss; it falls and shatters all over the floor. I quickly bend down to pick up the pieces before anyone finds out, only to kneel straight onto a huge shard that's sticking up. My scream is shrill and loud, that I'm sure frightens away every cockroach and dog in a three-mile radius. My mum comes hurtling out of the shower, stark naked and crying out 'What? What? What?' There is blood everywhere.

In the absence of bandages, she tears up my bed sheets, wraps them around my leg and races me up to the emergency department at the hospital. As we're waiting

Chapter 1 That's My Mum Onstage

there for what seems like hours, she distracts me by teaching me some songs, one of which is 'Que Sera Sera.'

> *When I was just a little girl,*
> *I asked my Mama, 'what will I be?*
> *Will I be pretty? Will I be rich?'*
> *Here's what she said to me:*
> *'Que Sera, Sera,*
> *Whatever will be, will be.*
> *The future's not ours to see.*
> *Que Sera, Sera.'*

A few weeks later, she will be dead.

I've just finished one of my weekend trips to see my dad at his farm near Gympie and we're waiting in the carpark at The Big Pineapple. I'm busting a gut to see my mum. If I'm lucky, once she gets here and handover is done, we'll go inside and get one of those decadent fruit parfaits in the sundae glasses with enough whipped cream on to ensure that the magnitude my anticipation matches my ensuing nausea. Either that, or she'll buy me an Ewok ice-block for the drive home.

We wait and wait, but she doesn't show.

FUNNY MUMMY

This is not normal. We walk up the inside of the Big Pineapple itself to kill some time, with my Dad's impatience seeming to grow with each step. He grumbles something about giving up and bloody hell and as if he didn't have a long enough drive back home.

We hop in the car and drive all the way back to Mum's house, where we find her lying in a makeshift bed set up in the lounge-room next to the TV. Dad is pissed off. Has she just forgotten about pick-up? It seems she has. Was she tired? Sick? Or worse?

He leaves in a huff and it's just the two of us. My mum and me. Ang is apparently staying with friends, though at the time I have no idea why, nor do I care. It's never just us. She puts out her arms for me and I climb into the bed next to her, our limbs wrapping around each other. I'm overjoyed to be back with her. We are home.

I chat happily and she smiles, running her hands through my as-always unkempt locks.

'Are you okay Mummy?' I ask. She seems fine, but it's not like her to be so immobile.

'I'm fine Wren, I just have a bit of a headache is all.'

Chapter 1 That's My Mum Onstage

I leap out of bed, cry 'I'll be right back' and skip into the kitchen. I return a minute later with a glass of water, walking carefully so I don't spoil my stunningly selfless moment by spilling it.

'Aww, you sweetheart,' she smiles, wriggling herself up a bit on the pillows so she can grasp it and have a sip.

I beam as I watch her – the most beautiful woman in the world – enjoying my five-year-old nursing prowess.

'All better?' I ask, feeling her forehead with my palm, just like she does for me when I am sick.

'Mmm-hmmm,' she nods, smiling and looking for where to put the water down. I grab it and carry it to the coffee table (I know what happens to carelessly placed glasses!), then jump straight back into bed next to her.

'Oh, you poor thing,' she says, 'you've hardly got any room.' She tries to edge over and make extra space but there's none to make; it's just a small mattress on a couch really. It's tiny.

'I'm fine Mummy, see?' I say, wrapping my legs around her waist, snuggling my head into her chest and holding my arms around her for dear life. I'm not sure how long we lay there together, just her and me, but I hope it was for a long time.

We are interrupted by the arrival of several of her friends, and I'm genuinely perplexed to see how worried they apparently are. They keep talking about how sick she is, how bad this is, and arguing with her about taking her to the hospital.

'Why?' I think. 'She only has a headache.'

The whole time they're discussing this I continue just lying next to her while she strokes my hair and protests the hospital plan.

'Why can't they just listen to her?' I think. 'Can't they just go? I've only just gotten home! I've been missing her for days! I've only just gotten her back to myself!'

Tom arrives. My stomach sinks, but not as far as usual, sure that with company around he'll be on his best behaviour. Within a minute, he uses his stubborn, misogynist assholery to do what I'll years later realise is probably the only good thing I ever saw him do for our family: he says, 'We are taking you to the hospital and that's that.'

Chapter 1   That's My Mum Onstage

I un-pry myself from her as he literally picks her up in his arms. I lie straight back down on the warmth where she's just been. I lie there as they shuffle towards the door, I lie there as she's carried past the door frame and out of sight, and I lie there afterwards, as I hear the Kombi van's motor start up, then fade away into the distance. I lie there and I lie there, and I lie there. She'd made room for me indeed. But I didn't want it.

There are no streetlights to keep me awake this time, but nonetheless I'll lay here until she returns, ready to surprise her and leap straight back into her arms.

For the next two weeks, my little sister and I stay with a lady named Jackie, with her three kids and her husband. Mum's 'headache', it turns out, was an aneurism; a blood vessel has burst inside her brain which is as not-good as it sounds. But right now, I have no idea what any of that means. All I know is that my mum is in hospital, in intensive care – and as such, no kids are allowed to visit, much to our distress. The eldest daughter, Naomi, is kind to me, and gives me free rein of her assortment of stickers, notepaper and craft supplies with which to make elaborate daily letters to send to my mum. She even shows me how to handmake envelopes to put them in, which I find gobsmackingly wonderful. I never get a reply from my Mum, but I'm assured it's only because she's too unwell to write but that she loves them and that she'll be back soon anyway.

One day I'm playing with the other kids in the garden when I fall into a rosebush. A thorn the size of an Ewok has lodged itself into my shin. I howl and wriggle and wail as Jackie tries to calm me down enough to get it out. After what seems like an eon, she smiles and says 'Look!' In a pair of tweezers, she holds the thorn triumphantly. 'See?' she says. 'Jesus got it out!'

I'm not a kid who swears, but I swear (pun intended) that what goes through my head is not far removed from, 'What the fuck are you talking about? Jesus didn't get it out. You did. I saw you!'

Spookily, it foreshadows a significant chapter of WTF-ery in my adult life, which I will spend in a marriage to a devout Christian, the extraction from which will require a great deal more than tweezers. But I'm getting ahead of myself. Again.

Every night I go to bed hoping against hope it is the last night without Mum, and that tomorrow will be the day she comes home, and we will get back to normal. Ballet lessons. Bike rides. Lying in bed with my feet between her legs, getting warmed up.

Chapter 1   That's My Mum Onstage

One morning I wake up and, lo and behold, it does mark the end of our time at Jackie's. But not to go back home; rather my grandma Laney and my uncle Doug, my Mum's mother and brother arrive to collect Ang and me and take us with them up to Laney's house in Toowoomba.

I have no idea what this means in terms of how Mum is going, but I know I'm relieved to at least be going somewhere familiar. I've been staying with Laney for weekends for as long as I can remember, and I love it. I get spoiled and get fed porridge and loads of toast and butter and it's somewhere that I don't have to worry about Tom's explosions, nor does Jesus unexpectedly appear from nowhere to help with minor first aid. It's predictable. It's family.

Another two weeks passes. Mum has still not answered one of my letters, but Laney says it's because one side of her body can't move so she can't write, no matter how much she wants to. Years later I'll be told that not only has my mother been paralysed down one side, but her short-term memory is all but non-existent. Visitors have left the room for a coffee and come back to find she has no memory of them having just been there. Meanwhile the doctors have been trying and trying to operate on the aneurism but every time they do, her brain goes into spasm.

It's been a month of not seeing our Mum. An eternity. A month of promises that she'll be home soon. A month of nights wondering if this will be the last one without her. A month of feeling like I'm back at that babysitter's house, lying in my bed and staring out at the streetlight below, waiting up all night for the car that might never come.

On July 4th, a month after she'd been carted off to hospital, she slips into a coma.

On July 7th, with no brain activity, they turn off her life support.

Everybody is in complete shock. Nobody ever dreamed this could happen. Well, aside from a doctor who had dared suggest a need to prepare the family for the possibility that things may not work out, to which my grandmother quickly shot back: 'Don't be ridiculous!'

And yet, the nightmare nobody had dared dream had arrived.

Laney told me many years later that when she saw my mum for the last time in the hospital just before the machines were turned off, her disbelief felt all the more profound.

Chapter 1 That's My Mum Onstage

'She didn't look sick at all, she just looked so peaceful. Like an angel. Just a sleeping angel.'

Of course, all of this drama has happened behind the scenes with Ang and me as yet oblivious to this tragic turn. We spend the afternoon of our mother's death watching a ballet at the Town Hall. It's magical and beautiful and one of the most marvellous things I've ever seen. For an hour and a half, nothing is wrong in the world, which I guess was exactly the experience Laney was hoping for – it was the last moments of our life where everything would be okay.

When we get home, my uncle asks me to come see him in the front bedroom. My memory of it is it being the middle of the night, as everything appears dark and blurry. Of course, this cannot be so; by all accounts, this happened in the middle of the afternoon, but the night-time is how I remember it. In fact, my memory of it is not even in my own body. I cannot recall his exact words, nor his face, nor my response. In my memory I'm floating above both of us, as though I'm on the ceiling looking down upon the top of our heads, and I watch benevolently as little Jenny on the bed cries and cries and cries as the currently remembering-this-Jenny-on-the-ceiling slowly fades away.

It's only years later that I realise that THAT afternoon, the one where it was just us two lying on the bed with her arms around me… that was our goodbye.

Chapter 2 It Takes a Retirement Village

You know how certain sights and smells take you back to childhood? Well for me, those include chook raffles, a really good red spot special and whenever I walk past incontinence pads in a supermarket. Depends All Nighters For Women? I'm a child again!

In a heartbeat, our life with my free-spirited muso mum at the beach is over. My sister and I move to Toowoomba to be raised by our grandmother. I never do dance classes again and I never strut my stuff as the blinged up piggy.

But as it turns out, ain't nothing gonna stop me from donning a stunning array of sequins at any given opportunity in my pursuit of becoming a shameless onstage ham.

From the age of five, I am suddenly thrust into the world of living among the elderly. Or specifically, the world of my grandmother 'Laney' – who will soon become known by both my sister and me as 'Mum' – and her community of aged friends.

Just as reflecting now that perhaps having the smells of beer and cigarettes and pubs so familiar to you as a young child is not the norm, it's only when I become an adult that I look back and realise that my childhood was actually pretty bizarre. You mean not EVERYBODY eats lamb's fry, bread and butter pudding, and bubble and squeak regularly? Not EVERYBODY spends a good chunk of their life at the RSL? (Note for the uninitiated: the RSL is the Returned and Services League, a support organisation for men and women who have served in the defence forces, famous for inexpensive counter meals and sense of community)? Not EVERYBODY has a medicine cabinet full of medications so old that they don't even have a label, yet alone a use-by date on them?

CHAPTER 2   IT TAKES A RETIREMENT VILLAGE

Not only is it, erm… unique being raised by an elderly woman, but so too is being thrust into the world that is her rather elderly friends. I guess you could say that much like Mowgli in the Jungle Book is raised by a pack of wolves, I am raised by a pack of geriatrics. Which given they both have a tendency to be grey, hairy and travel in packs, seems poetic. They say it takes a village to raise a child. Well in my sister's and my case, it takes a retirement village.

We spend umpteen hours accompanying her to lawn bowls, mah-jong, marching in Anzac Day parades, dining with the AWAS – those she served alongside in World War II from the Australian Women's Army Service. At the time, we could only guess this was some kind of secret women's club from her days in the army, but it now consisted of nattering and giggling over a pub meal. To my sister's and my delight, this includes drawing raffles which one of us mysteriously and wonderfully, always seemed to win.

So it is that in some bizarre near-time travel experience, we find ourselves being raised in the 1980s but with the attitudes and appearance of the 1940s.

We are being raised by an old person and all that comes with it: the way the house is kept (impeccable and smelling very much of mothballs and home cooking), the people who frequent our house for sherry and tea and roast dinners and cards and/or various combinations thereof, the way in which Mum dresses us, and most of all, her vehement hatred of wastage. She'd grown up through The Great Depression of course. 'Waste not, want not… Oh for that crust of bread that once I threw away!' is an oft-recited adage. I mean that literally. She recites it to us. Oft.

We have to clean every last trace of food off our plate, for if we don't, it will be glad-wrapped and put straight into the fridge, ready to be the next item to enter our mouths, even if it is the next morning. I quickly develop the strategy of wolfing down everything as quickly as possible to just get it over with; unfortunately, my sister doesn't catch on so fast and more often than not, finds herself sadly eating a breakfast of soggy green beans and carrots.

I think the most tangible example of bringing the past with me into this new life in Toowoomba is the presence of my long wild unruly, child-of-a-hippy, curly blonde hair. It had never experienced a haircut, was never brushed and I loved it.

A couple of weeks after we arrive, Laney takes me to visit her friend Glenys. Glenys lives on a little farm just outside of Toowoomba in a little pocket of the Darling Downs

Chapter 2 It Takes a Retirement Village

called Drayton. We arrive, I say a shy hello and then am invited to take a seat up on a tall stool while she covers me in a cape of sorts. I am confused but unafraid and any thoughts or feelings I have on the matter are immediately rendered irrelevant when suddenly, placed in front of my eager little face, is something I've never seen before: a humongous cream bun.

Coated with more sugar than a child should ingest in a month, it oozes deliciousness; I simply cannot believe my luck. My real mother had hugely restricted my exposure to such things; I lived the life up until now of salads and smoothies with the occasional Ewok ice block thrown in for a treat. So, a freaking cream bun was something I would never have even dared conceive of. These existed? Yes, they did. And one was right here in front of my delighted, ready chops.

I dive in. It is a dream. I eat, I nibble, I devour and when it is all gone, I lick my sugary lips in satisfaction and look up into the mirror.

I freeze.

My hair is gone.

One sugary cream bun later and I am a boy.

And thus, a lifetime pattern of ingesting copious amounts of sugar while simultaneously digesting emotional trauma is set in motion.

#PityMe

With my shocking early revelation that life was so impermanent, that it could end at any moment without warning, I become:

a) incredibly paranoid that everybody in my life will die; and
b) driven to do everything I can to imprint myself on the world.

I want to make a mark, to be remembered so that in doing so, I can cheat death. If your work outlives you, you become immortal in your own way, right?

I start recording little variety shows on my cassette recorder. I sing songs (terribly) that I've learned at school, most notably *Little Donkey* from our grade one Christmas play, I record 'meet Grade One!' segments where one by one, I impersonate each and every one of my classmates. I'm sure they would have been delighted.

Chapter 2 It Takes a Retirement Village

As I progress through school, I become an obsessive overachiever. I believe with every fibre of my being that as life is short, you should make the absolute most of each and every moment, every opportunity, and never look back with a smidgeon of regret that you could have tried harder. I am a straight A student, I win medals in swimming, gymnastics and athletics, I eventually become Head Girl (School Captain) as well as House Vice-Captain and President of Interact, our charity club. I say all this not to #HumbleBrag but rather to illustrate how completely insanely over-the-top my need to achieve was.

It is decades later that I watch a documentary about one of my favourite comedians, Eddie Izzard, called *Believe*. I had never known it, but it turns out that Eddie, too, had lost his mum suddenly when he was around the age of five. Then the mind-blowing bit: he too, had responded by becoming a chronic, and one might even say clinically diagnosed over-achiever, from doing stand-up in multiple languages, to running multiple marathons in succession (okay, so perhaps he had it even worse than I did.) But what hit me like a ton of bricks, was when, towards the end of the film, he sits on a couch in his old family home, and tearily realises that behind each of these things that he's doing, is the belief that if he keeps achieving, he'll somehow bring his mother back.

I still cannot watch that segment of the film without crying. I've never ever heard anybody on earth articulate so clearly exactly who I am and what I am doing with my life.

Many moons later, I am at an Eddie Izzard concert at the Queensland Performing Arts Complex in Brisbane. It's my birthday. I couldn't be happier. Except wait, turns out, yes, I can! Near the end of the show, Eddie announces that he'll be doing a free Q&A upstairs after the show.

I head upstairs along with a few hundred others, and soon Eddie emerges onto a small platform to cheers from the crowd and starts taking questions. The first few are all variations on 'can we take a selfie with you?' or 'Can I have a hug?' Eddie, trying to be patient but clearly a little exasperated, explains he doesn't want the Q&A to devolve into a night of hugs and happy snaps. Instead, he wants to respond to his audience's questions. He wants real connection, not something that could be put through an #InstaFilter. Hashtag Blessed.

I hold my arm up as high as I can be and lo and behold, he points to me. The woman in front mistakes it for her and says 'Me? Me?' The nice person in me wants to let her have it, but I KNOW it's meant for me. This is my shot. Eddie says 'No, the woman with the blonde hair behind you.'

Chapter 2 It Takes a Retirement Village

I take a deep breath as Eddie Izzard looks into my eyes across the crowded room.

'Eddie,' I say, 'I saw *Believe* and absolutely loved it. I too am a performer and lost my mother very young, and I've never felt anybody articulate so clearly what I went through as you did. I just wanted to ask you; do you feel at peace now about your mother's death?'

My heart is beating at a million miles per minute.

He answers: 'No, I don't think I'll ever be over it. I think about her every day…' He continues on and I'm ashamed to admit that in my hazy holy-shit-is-this-really-happening head state I can't remember the nuances of his reply. But it was something about knowing that he'll never be over it and that no matter what he achieves, it will be never be enough, but he's not going to stop doing it anyway. I wish I could recount it verbatim. Why the fuck didn't I think to record it? Because it was a moment I needed to be present in. And I was. And I still cannot believe it happened.

It takes days to come down. Not just because of this impossibly wondrous moment itself, but because it has finally fully hit me: MAGICAL SHIT ACTUALLY DOES HAPPEN. What else, I ask myself, might actually be possible in this crazy little life that I could never dare imagine?

But I digress. Back to the world of the elderly! Mum keeps the house locked up like a high security prison. She'd long before had bars installed on every window, double locks on the front and back doors (which absolutely HAD to be secured and locked at all times, even if you were inside the house), and would even make us lock our car doors whenever we were driving at night.

My uncle tells me years later this was actually for a logical reason, in her mind. Decades before, when she'd lived out on a property near St George, a nearby farmstead had been broken into and some men had done unspeakably disturbing violent acts on the mother of the household who was home alone at the time. They'd tied her up, beaten her and cut off her breasts. This is horrendous to hear now, when we're relatively desensitised to violence thanks to movies and TV, but this was the SIXTIES. Despite this obviously being an extremely rare occurrence in the world, the terror had struck Mum in the core of her being where it remained steadfast for the rest of her life.

To get to the spare key (if indeed, I was arriving home when she was out), we were under very strict instructions:

Chapter 2 It Takes a Retirement Village

> Walk around the back of the house, unhook the pool gate, go to the pool shed and undo the bolt on it.
>
> Open the door into the pool shed.
>
> Climb over everything (I'm not kidding, this procedure required Entrapment-style body contorting to navigate the piles of storage boxes) until you came to a tiny table.
>
> Under the table was a bowling bag.
>
> Behind that was a second bowling bag. Pick up the second one, open it.
>
> Down the bottom, under the bowling balls, was a tiny piece of fabric.
>
> Open up the fabric and there, neatly wrapped up inside, was the key.
>
> To the back door only.

It's quite shocking to think she doesn't rent a troll to ask us three questions.

And God help you if you don't put the key back EXACTLY where it belongs afterwards.

While many of my friends spend their weekends going with their family to the AFL (the Australian Football League) or the NRL (the National Rugby League) my sister and I spend a lot of ours at the RSL (the Returned and Services League).

We love the little old ladies that Mum convenes with and they love us. Every birthday they shower us with cards with a $2 coin or a Scratch-it taped inside.

And of course, we become wonderfully well versed in all the old-school war-time tunes, which later as adults, Ang and I will continue to celebrate in our acapella/cabaret group Betty and the Betties. Singing those songs really does lift your spirits.

Sometimes I can't believe that some of the world's most relentlessly optimistic, happy *Pack Up Your Troubles* type songs were written in the face of such awful, horrible and unimaginable tragic times. Was it even a good strategy? How could you even ask people to smile in the midst of so much darkness? But it begs the question then: what's the alternative? To just resign yourself to the darkness and only allow songs of sadness, horror and awfulness? To not sing at all? To give up and commit to your mental state embracing hopelessness?

Chapter 2   It Takes a Retirement Village

We can't change the shit that happens to us, or the world. But we can choose whether to laugh or cry.

We can choose to let our suffering destroy us or make us. We can choose to give up, or we can sing the damn war song.

Now while I may be painting a pretty cosy picture, shock horror: Mum wasn't perfect. She had faults. Many faults. As I grew up it distressed me. As I became an adult, while I could make more sense of it, I still held a grudge.

Years later I became a parent. And I forgave her EVERYTHING.

Holy. Freaking. Shitballs.

Parenting is the most exhausting, thankless and stressful experience I've ever been through. It takes everything out of you sometimes just to get through the day. And I am saying that being:

a)   a parent in my forties;
b)   partnered; (well, for some of it); and
c)   in relatively good health.

Mum, on the other hand, was:

a) starting again in her retirement;
b) single; and
c) in terrible pain almost all the time, thanks to dreadful arthritis in her back.

I had no idea then the extent of what she did for us – everything.

A week after my mother has died, I am out at the pool with my new 'Mum', sweeping with the pool brush while she scoops the little jasmine leaves out. Before I know what is happening, I plunge right in – in the middle of Toowoomba's freezing July, thrashing and flailing, the freezing water combining with the fact I can't swim fling me into a painful panic. Then I see it: the pole of the pool scoop outstretched to me, Laney urging me to grab it. Like a Hollywood movie, I grab the stick with melodramatic flair, and pull myself towards the edge where new-Mum wrenches me out. As I sit there spluttering and shivering, I gaze up into her eyes and utter the phrase which she will continue to recount with joy for the next several decades: 'You're my hero.'

I am astounded that not only did she take us on, but that she lost her temper as little as she did. And I came to the realisation that so long as you do your best, love them like crazy and do a 'good enough' job at raising kids, then guess what?

The shit bits won't matter.

The largest glaring hole in this new 'plan B' life with our grandmother is the absence of my big brother Jamie. He continues to live with his Dad, as he always did, but for some reason it takes years before we get to see each other again. This is devastating to think about, even now.

When the adults in our world finally get their shit together and organise a visit, I don't even recognise him. He's become a teenager. But then comes the laughter again. There he is. My clown. He reduces Ang and me to tears almost constantly; his visits on the occasional school holidays are the highlight of our year. It is him who I credit as my original comedy influence. Not only is he hilarious within his own right, but he has a voracious appetite for comedy, and it rubs off.

We watch dozens of comedy films at his suggestion and then crack up at his impersonations. He sends us a cassette tape where he's recorded us a personal radio show of sorts, where he's playing different characters complete with 'audience calls' again all played by himself. In our Mum's place, he has become the sun. And as it always had been, when it comes time for him to leave, I cry and cry and cry.

This huge injustice of separated siblings aside though, Mum does a pretty damn amazing job of giving us a good upbringing. She drives us to this activity and that activity. She packs thousands of lunch boxes. Including ones with – for some reason – vegemite and lettuce sandwiches, but enough about the gag reflex. She cooks umpteen meals. She does so many things to keep our lives going, so covertly, aside from the occasional 'I'm not appreciated!' tantrum, that when I do finally move out, it is genuinely shocking to me when my share house bathroom gets dirty. It was always clean at home. Something is clearly wrong here. We should call the landlord! The sink is gathering dust, dirt and grime, and let's not even talk about the toilet floor. Contact the RTA immediately to discuss my tenanting rights!

But from those first unthinkable, unsteady days of having two little sad girls thrust into her own grief-soaked world full-time, Mum puts one foot in front of the other until over a decade has passed and by God, she's bloody done it. She's done what had seemed impossible all those years ago.

Chapter 2 It Takes a Retirement Village

The day I leave for uni, I am a blubbering mess, along with my sister, but to my surprise, Mum is uncharacteristically stoic. As we say goodbye, I cling to her like teenage John Connor to the Terminator, while she coolly pats me on the back.

'Just don't touch alcohol,' she says. 'Promise me you won't.' 'Okay,' I sniffle.

'Promise me, Jenny.' She looks me in the eye. She hadn't done all she'd done over the past decade and a bit to just 'throw me to the wolves', as she put it. 'Promise me.'

'I promise.'

I leave, travel the three hours to commence my very first night of university life and ring home to do our traditional 'I just called to say I love you' serenade. At least I think I do. I can't be sure.

I am pretty drunk.

Chapter 3 When Following Your Dreams Is So Exciting Your Period Stops

L ike many young munchkins in 1984, I am obsessed with Star Wars. I have an Ewok lunchbox. I dress in my Mum's flowing white hippy dress at every opportunity and bam! I'm Princess Leia. My best childhood friend Pablo and I grab onto the rope swing hanging from the beams under my house, I whisper, 'Good luck' and we swing. And we get rope burn. To my delight, every lunch break at kindergarten goes far too quickly thanks to the entire class being obsessed with playing Stormtroopers.

FUNNY MUMMY

I play with complete and utter devotion.

I BELIEVE IT.

One day somebody shoots me with a laser blaster, and I commit to a highly dramatic death… falling on the top of a hill, rolling down it and finally stopping with my eyes shut and my body frozen. I don't move. Minutes pass, me waiting for somebody to come to my aid, to try to wake me up, anything. Nothing. Exasperated, I open my eyes slowly, to see about a dozen four-year-old heads around me in a circle, looking at me worriedly.

And while the words don't hit me at that moment, in some non-literal form, the realisation hits me.

I AM A PERFORMER.

As I grow, the dream never leaves me.

I will be a serious dramatic actor. I will do character pieces with or without prosthetics, that move everybody to tears and are talked about in hushed tones for decades to come. I will start my Oscar speech with 'I'd like to thank my husband, Johnny Depp…'

Chapter 3 When Following Your Dreams Is So Exciting Your Period Stops

(This was, naturally, well before the future hubby of my dreams was to reveal himself to be not just a hot man but also a hot mess.)

What I'm saying is, if you look up 'grounded' in the dictionary, I'm pretty sure it says, 'the opposite of Jenny Wynter.'

I perform in every play I can. I take drama lessons. I avidly follow the careers of those I admire. I get the brochures on drama schools.

And my Mum is mortified.

'I always said that my Jenny,' she would say in front of company, presumably so I can argue less, 'should be in business or law.' I want neither.

So, without telling her, I tick 'Film and Television' on my university application form. It's not acting, but it's the next best thing, and with my other major being Marketing, it appeases her enough to feign support.

I finish my degree, and decide to take a semester off, which then turns into an entire year when I fall in love and become a besotted bum. Tim is the big brother of my sister's bestie; both gals have joked for some time about setting us up. We quickly become completely smitten. We are so young. So baby faced. So unaware of how small issues can become big issues. So sure that love is enough.

Which is why we get engaged.

Yet we make few moves towards actually organising the wedding. We finally sit down and have a heart to heart: neither of us feels ready. Wait, NEITHER of us?

Oh thank God!

We break up.

I'm now 22 years old and single.

Now what?

> *I've spent this life being such a good, good girl*
> *But now I'm seeing things in a different kind of way,*
> *It's like all these years I've been on a strict one-man diet,*
> *And now I'm standing at an all-you-can-eat buffet…*
> *So let's dig in!'*
> — Let's Dig In! from my cabaret
> *An Unexpected Variety Show*

CHAPTER 3   WHEN FOLLOWING YOUR DREAMS IS SO EXCITING YOUR PERIOD STOPS

And so, I do dig in. I hurl myself at the serve-yourself buffet of young men in the world like a starving country girl who's never seen Sizzler and literally dry humps the salad bar.

It's delicious and fun and I go back many times until I need a lie down and a good antacid.

Now what? What do I even want from life? Oh yeah, to FOLLOW MY WILDEST ACTING DREAMS DANGFLAMMIT!

As brilliant as this care-free hook-up focused chapter of my life is, I know deep down that I want more than strangers to love me one on one. I want an audience.

On a total whim, I decide to move to Sydney.

I will finally go for what I'd always wanted: I will become an *Alec Guinness voice* ACT-OR. I have no job. I have no money. I have no plan. But I don't need anything.

I. Am. An. Artist.

I move into a tiny upstairs room of an acquaintance who just so happens was needing a flatmate. Serendipity! The stars are aligned! I am fulfilling my destiny! (As it turned out, said acquaintance apparently ALWAYS has a need for a flatmate, as he is such a pain in the arse to live with that he has a continually rotating roster of people who've had it up to here with him. But that's another story…)

I enrol in a physical theatre class, which in hindsight, is kinda ridiculous given I had zero aspirations to be a theatre performer, physical or otherwise, and was all about the screen. But… the course was the cheapest I could find.

I send out resumes to all of the acting-related organisations I can, thinking that if I could start working for them in admin and/or marketing, that would be a foot in the door to impressing them with my acting potential! As you can see, this was an incredibly well thought out plan, jampacked with logic. We all know that Meryl Streep was discovered when she was doing data entry for Uta Hagen.

Right?

RIGHT!

I get a job working for The Actors' Centre. BAM! Fortune is favouring me! Sure, I'm doing front of house for their student graduating showcase, but I'm rubbing shoulders with actual, genuine, real life acting students! It is less of a big break and more of a mild sprain, but I am floating on air. I have arrived!

CHAPTER 3 WHEN FOLLOWING YOUR DREAMS IS SO EXCITING YOUR PERIOD STOPS

I go to auditions! Any auditions. For a theatre restaurant an hour and a half's commute away, for a rock covers band where I know about three songs from their playlist and for the National Institute of Dramatic Arts. I don't get any of them. But them's the breaks, right?!

I can do it!

All of this time I've been feeling very crampy and awaiting my inevitably impending period. I go to the bathroom, convinced this is it, but then… nothing.

I've been taking naps during the daytime, which is incredibly unlike me. But I am exhausted from all of my auditioning. All of this creative energy leaves you depleted and nanna-like. Right?

It is my new flatmate Tamsin who says to me 'Is there any chance you could be pregnant?' What?!

NO! No way.

I wait another week. And another week.

'I'm going to go to the doctor,' I tell Tam. 'Do you reckon you'd be willing to- '

'What time?' she says.

We stroll up the street together to the local GP, me babbling on about how I wasn't pregnant but if I was, which I wasn't, then it was a no-brainer, I'd have an abortion and move on with my life. But I wasn't, so I wouldn't, so it wasn't an issue. If it was positive, which it wouldn't be, I wouldn't be upset, I'd be unemotional, robot-like and just get on with doing what had to be done. But I wasn't. No way.

I go in. I pee into a jar. I go back into the doctor's office and hand it to him. He puts a strip in and having done a pregnancy test years before – thankfully negative – I am used to waiting the requisite 3 minutes for results, so brace myself for a long and awkward silence between us.

Within two seconds he says, 'That's come up positive right away.'

The world stops.

I burst into tears.

He hands me tissues and asks what my situation is.

'I have to – I have to have an abortion.'

Chapter 3 When Following Your Dreams Is So Exciting Your Period Stops

He just looks sad – or is that me? – and reaches into a drawer and rummages around for a business card. He hands it to me, explains something something counselling something something phone them something something and with that I leave.

I walk into the waiting room and Tamsin looks up at me expectantly. I just nod and her face falls, and I burst into another round of sobs.

We saunter back with her arm around me, and stop in at the cafe opposite our house – the one I walked by every day and swooned over the smells inside, promising myself I'd finally go in there once I landed an acting gig and could afford more than just bread, potatoes and the odd vegetable, and order a massive pizza.

I cry between munches, bemoaning my shame, when Tamsin says 'You know, having an abortion is fine if that's what you want, but I think down the track you're going to want to look back and know that you actually thought through the options properly.'

'Yes,' I nod. 'You're right.'

'So, let's think it through. One option: you could have a baby… another op-'

I nearly splutter. 'No, I couldn't. I can't possibly. I have no job, I have no money, I have no partner.'

'I'm not saying you should,' she says. 'I'm just saying, you could.'

I could? I could!? I COULD!

Okay, so it took a little more than five seconds to make one of the biggest decisions of my life, but the point is, I decided that HOLY SHIT I WAS GOING TO HAVE A BABY.

Spoiler alert: it turns out that a one-night stand can actually become a lifetime commitment, at least for one party. #WhoKnew? But I didn't have time to really process the politics of this for now because did I mention that HOLY SHIT I WAS GOING TO HAVE A BABY.

I would be amazing at it. I would be a strong, kick ass woman, fearlessly traversing the globe and following my greatest dreams with a baby on my back. Or front. Or side. Basically, any which way, depending on which sling I could afford. Nothing would stop me!

Long story short... after this, Tim and I reunite. We decide to have the baby together, raise it as ours. Insane, I know. This crazy life event has finally made us realise that we

Chapter 3 When Following Your Dreams Is So Exciting Your Period Stops

don't want to say goodbye forever; we want to be together no matter what. We will rise above. This will make us stronger.

We get married on the beach at dawn. An elderly man trudges through the middle of our ceremony wearing nothing but a pair of budgie smugglers[2].

True romance.

As my belly grows, so does my resolve that come hell or high-water, NOTHING is going to keep me from my dreams. I will be one of those funky mums you see out and about at festivals, baby in the sling, business at the front, party down the back! Oh wait, no that's a mullet.

Anyhoo, I will be a mother AND be fabulous. Nothing will change!

Everything changes.

---

[2] Aussie slang for Speedos, also known as 'dick togs', 'DTs', or 'that which should never be worn.'

Firstly, childbirth.

Holy shit. I've been eagerly awaiting labour, looking forward to the challenge of it, sure that it will be an experience I wanted to observe, to write about, to HOLY MOTHER OF BOWIE MAKE IT STOP NOW!

I think it sums up the experience here: when I have to get transferred from my quiet and lovely Birth Centre Suite into a medical delivery room because the baby's heart rate has dropped dangerously low, my only thought is 'I HOPE IT'S BAD ENOUGH THAT THEY CUT HER OUT OF ME.' These are not the thoughts of a happy woman.

She arrives safe and sound, disaster is averted, and I am of course, forever changed.

My beautiful little munchkin, Ella. She melts me. Her little possum eyes, her perfectly untouched velvet skin, I marvel at how nothing in the world has hurt her yet.

I have a whole lifetime to fuck her up.

"I should pace myself", I think.

Chapter 3   When Following Your Dreams Is So Exciting Your Period Stops

When she is three days old, I sit on the rocking chair in our lounge room nursing her, when all of a sudden, I burst into sobs of grief. Images of my mum flooded my postnatal mind. My whole life, I'd seen her death as a total tragedy for my sister and me, but here I am, for the first time ever, as I stare at my innocent little baby, realising the dreadful loss that SHE experienced. Only now do I realise fully how tremendously she loved me. And here and now, I know that the worst thing I could possibly imagine would be not being there to see my little girl grow up. The real tragedy, I realise, was my mother's.

A year or so later we go back to the buffet for seconds… a little boy, Caleb. De-freaking-licious. I am bowled over by how much I adore my babies. I want to inhale them. Glue is easier, so I go with that (JK!)

My body changes. People don't tend to realise this, but after you give birth, you actually still look pregnant. For, you know, ever. While I strive to be body positive, I still to this day will have moments where I catch myself in the mirror and feel like a badly-burned landlord who's evicted tenants from hell. I want to scream 'This is not the original condition of the premises! I can prove it! I have photos! Now GET BACK HERE AND FIX THIS SHIT UP!'

But you know, loves of my lives totes worth it blah blah blah.

Chapter 4 I'm Being A Vagina And They Hate Me

So, you may have noticed that I had two children under the age of two, which in another dialect of English roughly translates to 'I was losing my mind.' In a random conversation with my sister-in-law's new boyfriend, it comes up how I used to love acting but now I have my hands full with kids, but how I find myself still pining for the stage.

'Oh wow,' he says. 'Actually, a mate of mine has just started up an improv night in West End, I'm pretty sure they're looking for performers. Do you want me to give you his number?' IMPROV.

YES.

I'd done bits and pieces at school and completely loved it. I knew you had to just agree with whatever the other person said onstage, and to be honest, I'd be so elated just to have a valid reason to be out of the house that I would have happily agreed with what anybody said offstage as well.[3]

I call up, I audition, and a week later I find myself onstage – well, on the floor, really – at a super casual and probably incredibly dodgy quality improv sports night at the Melbourne Hotel. We are paid with a pub meal and two beers. I HAVE ARRIVED.

I am seriously in heaven. A night of performing! I don't have to rehearse, and despite the fact that our gigs are pretty far from world class improvised comedy, I begin to grow confidence that I could be funny. People are laughing.

Without this little taste of affirmation, I doubt I would have had the courage for what comes next: I see a sign on a noticeboard calling for entrants to the Triple J Raw Comedy

---

[3] This is not a safe philosophy in showbiz!

Chapter 4 I'm Being A Vagina And They Hate Me

Competition. I don't have a scrap of material. I don't have any idea what I would even talk about. But I call up and enter immediately. I know that with an actual deadline, it will force me to come up with something!

I come up with about five minutes of stuff which I practise on my sister, who'd always done a bloody brilliant job at laughing at all of my jokes. I am so terrified, that I decide to do something which in hindsight is probably insane: I take a guitar onstage with me to do some musical stuff, despite the fact I'VE NEVER PLAYED A GUITAR IN FRONT OF ANYBODY.

When it comes time to soundcheck, I don't even know how to plug it in. As the sound guy realises this, he gives me a look that says 'Oh. Shit.'

But... I do a few musical gags and an incredibly lame parody of 'Cats in the Cradle' about having children, and with my guitar feeling like a shield between me and the audience, I feel relatively safe. Plus, I figure, at least this way even if they don't laugh at me, they'd listen.

To my surprise, it goes really well. I get through to the semi-final, and then to the final, which I do not win but holy shit I am hooked!

FUNNY MUMMY

Afterwards, Fedele Cristi, who runs the Sit Down Comedy Club in Brisbane, comes up to me and says 'You should keep going. Give me a call and we'll sort you some open mics.'

And thus, from that point onwards, Mummy is out of the house multiple nights a week to strut her stuff.

I start doing longer sets and getting paid. Meagrely, but at the time, with kids and a full-time student for a husband, $50 and a free beer feels like a windfall.

One paid gig a week soon turns into several, and before I know it, I seem to have the beginnings of an actual career in this thing. I can't believe it.

Family during the day, comedy at night! The perfect combination! You CAN have your dreams and your family!

With Tim studying externally, we have a bit of flexibility as a family, and so it is that we embark on an adventure together to Melbourne International Comedy Festival!

We house-sit a friend's place and try to make a family holiday of it, which, with two young children, is no mean feat. Then come night-time, I venture off into the city to do

Chapter 4 I'm Being A Vagina And They Hate Me

as many guest spots and see as many shows as I can squeeze in.

The day we fly in I get a message from Josh Thomas (yes, THAT Josh Thomas... of P*lease Like Me* and Netflix's *Everything's Gonna Be Okay* fame – we'd met at Triple J's Raw Comedy competition, which he went on to win, and he'd been awesome to me: inviting me to perform regularly at his new room at Brisbane Powerhouse) asking if I'd like to be his plus one at the Comedy Fest Opening Gala Party that night. Uh... hells to the yes?!

And so it is that I walk into the first party that makes my head explode. To a little starstruck nobody who's been doing comedy for five minutes, this is like a tantalising sneak behind the curtains of what I think I want, a little snapshot of what could possibly be. Josh and I keep gasping and quietly squealing at each other over what seems to be an entire ballroom crammed full of the big-name comedians in the Aussie scene. Tim Minchin. Rove McManus. Daniel Kitson. Corinne Grant. Arj Barker. Dave Hughes. Eddie Perfect. Wil Anderson. I could name a gazillion more.

'I wonder if one day,' I muse to Josh, 'we'll be in here and some young comics will be going 'Oh wow, there go Jen and Josh!''

Of course, that comes true for Josh a few years later. But not for *holding hand dramatically over forehead* MEEEEEE……!!!!!

Over the duration of the festival, I realise that in terms of my little comedy career, I have a long way to go. I only have about ten minutes of useable material thus far. In my deluded head, because I can get onstage and be confident this material works, I have arrived. I should add here that I think anybody starting out in comedy has to possess a level of delusion – if you don't then why would you bother keeping going when it can be such a harsh first year or two while you suck and improve and suck and improve some more? I know so many brilliant improvisers who've tried stand-up and quit after one or two gigs. I think it's for the best. If you're not prepared to suck for at least a year then you really shouldn't be doing it. Comedy certainly doesn't need more comedians; I think it's a natural weeding out process of the committed.

But back to the problem of the 10 minutes. Aside from the fact that I don't yet have nearly enough stage time to know how to handle different situations, I don't yet possess enough MATERIAL to handle different audiences. Nowadays, I might sketch out a set order. However, if I walk into a comedy gig and throughout the evening determine that *this* bit probably isn't going to resonate with

Chapter 4 I'm Being A Vagina And They Hate Me

a single, childless crowd, or that there's a particular audience member the MC has chatted with who has an interest in tennis (and I happen to have a great bit about tennis), then I can adjust accordingly. To stack the deck in my favour, if you will.

But back then... NUP.

Which is how I end up performing my childbirth song *One Night in Labour* (a parody of *One Night in Bangkok*) in front of one table of rather elderly people. They are the only people in the free comedy room, who've presumably just ventured out for a nice pub meal together and instead are being assaulted with an open mic line-up. It is during the part of my song when I start re-enacting a child coming out of the birth canal, that I realise the error of my ways. In this part of the act, I usually have guaranteed guffaws, but instead this time: crickets. My epiphany hits me hard. *I'm being a vagina and they hate me*. I suddenly start giggling and can't stop. I giggle through the final verses of the song, shrug my shoulders and leave the stage. It is the first time I've bombed terribly yet not been terribly upset about it. I learn a valuable lesson and gain a great story for my memoirs. LEMONADE. And, you're welcome.

Immersing myself in the festival is amazing, it is exhausting and by the end of it I'm not sure if comedy is for me. I love the art of it, I love the actual doing of it, but the relentless exhaustion… particularly when doing it while looking after small children for the rest of the time, well… it just seems like a massive mountain in front of me and while it's possible to climb it, I'm just not convinced I want it enough to justify the effort involved I decide to take a break. Is comedy breaking me?

A few months without performing, then I will reassess.

A week later, I pull into my driveway, groceries in my arms, and pull a letter out of the letterbox which I begin to open on the walk upstairs:

> *'Dear Ms Wynter,*
> *I am pleased to inform you that you have been awarded a Lord Mayor's Fellowship for New and Emerging Artists to the value of $15,500 to travel to the USA to undertake intensive training in improvised comedy.'*

I'm not joking when I tell you I literally drop the milk which proceeds to spill all over the stairs, and then I cry.

I CRY OVER SPILLED MILK.

Chapter 4   I'm Being A Vagina And They Hate Me

I've decided to take a break and instead, I've been given one.

A couple of months later, I say goodbye to my children at the airport for three and a half weeks of an absolute dream of an opportunity, working with Second City and the like in New York, Boston, Las Vegas and LA.

While I've been squealing with excitement and joy at this unbelievable dream come true, and have managed to organise for my sister to move in as nanny the whole time, the moment I walk through the departure gate my stomach lurches and I began to inwardly whine like a dog who's fretting over her puppies. Is this all a terrible mistake? What the hell am I doing? What kind of mother leaves her young children behind for a month? What if the plane crashes and I never see them again? Would I deserve it? Is this what I get for abandoning them? I am so selfish; how could I possibly have ever thought this was a good idea?

I spend the first ten days of the trip bawling my eyes out.

I try to cheer myself up my first night in NYC by walking through Times Square and down Broadway. It definitely helps! Note to everybody: do this whenever you're feeling down. However, every selfie I have of that night is of me looking exhausted, bloodshot and post-cry.

I'm in Las Vegas airport, mustering every ounce of strength I can to not burst into tears. It's 2.45am. I have caught the red-eye flight from NYC, I am starting training in musical improv at Second City at 9am and I've just missed my shuttle bus from the airport. The next one is in 30 minutes. Not a big deal, but it's 2.45am. 2.45. AM. In the morning. Did I mention it's 2.45am?

I feel like I'm going to collapse. Somehow that half an hour passes, the shuttle bus arrives and, like a ray of sunshine I need so desperately, there she is: Shirley. A middle-aged African American woman, Shirley is so perky and courteous and welcoming that for a moment it feels like it is not the god-awful middle of the night at all but a beautiful spring morning. She is the closest thing I've ever met to an American Julie Andrews.

'Why hello ma'am,' she warmly smiles, as I slowly trudge on board. It becomes clear quickly that Shirley takes immense pride in her job. It's not that she takes her role as shuttle driver seriously so much as she takes it upon herself to promote her title to that of 'tour guide.'

Chapter 4 I'm Being A Vagina And They Hate Me

Once I and my fellow red-eye flight budget travellers are settled, she launches into a beaming spiel of epic pride in her hometown in a voice that is as authoritative as it is excited.

'Now the hotels you see ahead appear to be very close together,' she says, her enunciation impeccable as though every single word is as important as the next. 'That is because they are very large!' She stretches out the final word LAAAAARGE.

'Nearly every day we have tourists who think they can walk from one hotel to the other but when they realise how far it actually is and how hot it is outside; they literally pass out from the heat.'

We do the obligatory 'MMMMM...' and 'REALLY?'s.

'But they usually just call the paramedics, and they just give them some water and some smelling salts and they're usually okay.'

'SO!' She adds, in a 'and-the-moral-of-the-story-is' kind of voice, 'if you do decide to walk, make sure you take a backpack with you and just throw in some water and some smelling salts.'

Aaaaariiiight. So your unconscious limb can reach in and grab the necessary tools to revive you?

As it happens, I am the final drop-off passenger on Shirley's bus. With her formal tour complete we just chat as she drives.

She tells me how much she loves Atlanta, her *real* hometown, and how she wishes that she and her family could move back there, as all of her family and her friends and everybody in the world who she loves is there.

'So, what brought you out here?' I ask.

'Oh,' she says as matter of fact as if I asked her what she was cooking for breakfast the next morning, 'we just came out here to win the jackpot.'

I was confused. She meant metaphorically right? Was saying it like that an Americanism?

'The jackpot?' I ask.

'You know… on the slot machines.'

It hits me. Oooohhhhh. This was what brought people here. The chance at a better life. Not a better life here but that this

Chapter 4 I'm Being A Vagina And They Hate Me

would be a stepping stone to the life they really wanted. There were people like this in the world who would stake everything, even the chance to live with the people they actually loved, in the place that they actually wanted to live, for a lottery ticket in the sweepstakes for a dream life.

Talk about a mirage in the desert.

'So how long have you been out here?' I ask.

'Oh,' she says. 'it's coming up around 23 years.' What the actual fuck?

'Oh,' I said. 'Wow.'

23 years? TWENTY-THREE YEARS?! I've had dreams that lasted less than 23 seconds. And here she is telling me she and her husband have forgone the life they actually want for a ticket in the draw.

I am yet to realise that my propensity to invest my family's money in comedy Festival shows is indeed akin to having a gambling problem. I am a gambler in denial, just like Shirley, so invested in this path, so far down the rabbit hole that I couldn't walk away if I tried and there was every possibility that in 23 years, I too, would be trying to remain cheerful, driving along and still waiting to win the jackpot.

Sure, the more effort you put in, the more gigs you do; the more social media and networking you do, the more festival invitations flowed in; the more momentum you get going, the more tickets you have in the draw. But if I've learned anything from my childhood years at the RSL, it's that even having a lot of tickets in a raffle doesn't guarantee you the chook.

Chapter 5 You Know, If You Wanna Stay in Canada Forever, It's Real Easy...

U pon my return from the USA, the entire world has opened up. I've learned from some of the best in the world, Goddamnit.

The world feels magical, electric... and for the first time since walking into that doctor's office and peeing on a stick, EVERYTHING FEELS POSSIBLE.

I beg Tim to take our little family overseas. Absolutely for my own selfish reasons, but I also feel genuinely convinced – and do to this day – that travel is an incredible experience for children. He finally agrees and so it is that we begin to sculpt a plan for an epic family adventure abroad! In my ideal world we'd move to NYC but practically speaking, financially and logistically, that's just not going to happen. The UK? As a teacher, getting a job for Tim is the easy part. Getting a visa for me and the kids? Not so much. And then, it hits us: Canada.

Oh Canada! She with her stunning mountainous landscapes! She with her booming comedy scene! She with her extremely-easy-to-get visas!

My hubby has one request: that before we move to the bright lights of Vancouver or the hubble bubble (that's a thing, right? Yes, that's a thing) of Toronto, we go somewhere quiet, somewhere small, somewhere we can just focus on being a family.

And so it is that in August 2007 we make our way towards the charming little Canadian town of Canmore.

At LAX airport, where we are only planning to be for a grand two hours between connecting flights, we are

Chapter 5 You Know, If You Wanna Stay in Canada Forever, It's Real Easy...

interrogated about 'the purpose of our visit' so aggressively we begin questioning the purpose of our lives.

At Calgary airport, the immigration lady takes one look at us, stamps our passports and says with a cheeky grin, 'You know, if you wanna stay in Canada, it's REAL easy!'

Our Canadian love affair has begun.

As our jet-lagged little family buses its way from Calgary towards Banff, and the landscape changes from plainlands to mountains, it's all I can do not to squeal out loud. It's like being in a dream. We pull up to the Banff Centre for the Arts, where we'll be staying in their hotel for our first week until our sublet apartment in Canmore, some 20 minutes away, is ready.

The Bow Valley (combining Banff and Canmore) is so ridiculously stunning picturesque that it's almost nauseating. Everywhere you turn there is a trillion-dollar view of the magnificent mountains, standing victorious over the lush pine forest. After nearly a year of preparations and saving and feeling like this day would never actually come, here it is. And it is already beyond my wildest dreams.

Like making drunken eye contact across a dancefloor, when it comes to Canada, it is illogical lust at first sight. (Okay, so there's no way I can ever know if it was reciprocated but, in my mind, me and Canada are on like Donkey Kong!) This is like walking unsteadily towards that attractive stranger in the nightclub and realising to your delight that they're even better close up.

I think I giggle with giddy delight every day for the first three months. Our sublet is an adorable Swiss chalet style A-frame, over two levels with the dining room framed by a massive glass window with the most stunning mountain view I've ever seen. We make breakfast, turn on the French kids' TV channel (a good educational opportunity, I figure), and I stare at that view grinning like an idiot and pinching myself.

The only downside of this new life is: Canmore, gorgeous as it is, has zero comedy scene. And we have zero friends. But, with no other option than to hang out together, as a family we throw ourselves into this new world. We're drinking way too much hot chocolate, ice-skating with Santa on the pond (Ella nearly takes him out), bike-riding, hiking…

Chapter 5 You Know, If You Wanna Stay in Canada Forever, It's Real Easy...

I quickly discover a bittersweet truth: that for the first time I feel like I'm finally enjoying my kids rather than enduring them.

Of course, while we venture out and savour the sights of our newfound life, there is the pressing concern of Tim and I finding jobs before our savings run out. Fortunately, the entire state of Alberta at this time is in a construction boom, so much so that they've been 'importing' workers from Mexico just to keep up with demand. Within a week, Tim begins working with a construction company, who are so desperate for workers they are happy to train him on the job.

Being the stay at home parent, I am more than a little limited in the hours I could work: but somehow, I find a job that not only fits our schedule, but also happens to fulfil my high school dream at the same time: working in a video store. (A video store – think of it being like Amazon Prime or Netflix, but in boxes.) Avalanche Movie is something of a local icon in the Bow Valley thanks to its most excellence lenience on late fees and free help-yourself popcorn while you browse. The pay is utter shit – $10 an hour, which after having just recently begun getting $200 plus a night for a comedy gig, is a MASSIVE lesson in humility – but the management and the staff are utterly brilliant.

It is FUN!

And, as an incredible bonus, it just so happens that Avalanche has the BIGGEST COLLECTION OF STANDUP COMEDY DVDs I would ever see in a video store. As in, hundreds of them. Every night, once my shift is done, I pick a bundle of DVDs, bring them home and watch them until the early hours of the morning. To me, that is my real wage. Tim says I spent that year putting myself through comedy college.

I watch a doco on Billy Crystal, who recounts a moment early in his career when he and his new agent went to a stand-up comedy night and watched a guy slay (Note to non-comedy folks: 'Slay' is good. Very good.)

Afterwards, Billy turned to his agent and commented on how great that was.

'Yeah,' said the agent, 'but he didn't leave a tip.'

'Huh?' said Billy.

'Well, it was funny and entertaining but I'm not gonna walk out of here with anything to think about, nothing. He didn't leave a tip.'

Chapter 5   You Know, If You Wanna Stay in Canada Forever, It's Real Easy...

That still stays with me. Ironically, *that* is the tip.

Another DVD is about a famous Canadian comedy duo, Wayne and Shuster, who became absolutely huge in comedy at the time. So naturally, Hollywood came knocking. However, the pair decided to turn down the opportunities there, quite happy with their lives as they were. 'What?!' screamed an LA agent down the phone. 'There's more to life than being happy!'

I am stoked to score a sweet gig on the side writing a weekly column for the two local papers; the *Banff Crag and Canyon* and the *Canmore Leader*. They give me free rein to write about all of my new experiences as an Aussie parent experiencing life in the Bow Valley. It pays little more than pocket money, but still, I can't believe my luck in scoring a gig that gives me some sort of comedy outlet and an avenue for documenting the everyday adventures with the kids in this new life.

Often the most painful parenting moments make for the best writing, like the column about my son throwing a massive public tantrum cross country skiing. He is outraged, OUTRAGED, I tell you, at having to wear pants in the snow. I push on, only to finally have him run inside the ski lodge, and for me to walk inside to find him in the very centre of the dining room, stripped off to his undies, looking triumphant. Moral of the story? What's bad for life is good for comedy. Plus, I find huge relief for my mental health in knowing that any awful real-life moment is excellent for the column. #Therapy #Recommended #FindAnOutlet

It is around this time that I first enter the doors of what I would come to know as 'The Moose', or as it's formally known, Loose Moose Theatre Company. I'd heard of it for years. It's famous within the improv world, in no small way due to its founder, Keith Johnstone, who is widely known as the creator of Theatre Sports™.

Before I'd left Australia, I'd applied and been accepted into the Loose Moose International Summer School the following year, but given that I now live down the road (well, an hour and a bit down the road in the Rocky Mountains, but still, quite a bit closer than Brisbane, Australia), I am able to venture in every Saturday and join their weekly company class.

I have no idea as I first drive into that nondescript car park, walk up their stairwell, through the foyer and into that theatre that I have just found my comedy heart and home. That one day, when I've long since left to return to Australia, I'll be dreaming of this place and waking up crying.

Chapter 5   You Know, If You Wanna Stay in Canada Forever, It's Real Easy...

But for now, it is just an exciting place where I find my tribe, quickly make friends and get to play in class and onstage in front of an audience.

The first ever class though, shocks me. I can't believe how harsh the feedback is. There is rarely a 'this was good' type comment, but rather what feels like an onslaught of negativity on all the things that had gone wrong.

My experience of 'feedback' at improv shows in Brisbane was that we NEVER spoke of the negative; we'd only offer positive feedback on what we liked. Loose Moose culture shock slapped me in the 'Yes, and…'

BUT within a couple of classes, I quickly realise that this feedback is:

a) Blunt and direct, but aimed at your performance, not you as a human being;
b) Not personal: every single improviser is given it the same way and
c) A **really** efficient way to get better.

I decide that my desire to keep my ego unbruised is far outweighed by my need to get better. I want to become the best improviser and performer I can possibly be; I know I am in exactly the right place to help me achieve that and so,

I put my pride aside and decide to get on with it. I do as many classes as I can, play in as many shows as I can make – often with my kids either in the audience or hanging with their Dad in the games arcade at the back of the building – and slowly but surely, I get better.

The following year I do the International Summer School and it is one of the most incredible learning experiences of my life. A dozen or so improvisers from all over the world join up for two weeks of seven hours of improvisation classes every single day, taught by two of the best teachers in the world, Dennis Cahill and Shawn Kinley. To this day, I adore them both. I can honestly credit anything good I ever do onstage to them.

They teach me how – and why! – to fail, not just graciously, but happily. How to relax enough onstage so that your natural charm can come through without having to try so hard. How to really connect with an audience. How to be more playful and really enjoy being onstage. How to stop taking yourself so goddamn seriously. In other words, incredibly important lessons for improv and indeed, for life.

They also teach me to remember what a privilege it is just to be onstage. In 2018, after nearly a decade away from Canada, I finally return with my kids to visit. I park in that big nondescript car park, walk up that stairwell, through

Chapter 5 You Know, If You Wanna Stay in Canada Forever, It's Real Easy...

that corridor and into that theatre and every fibre of my being squeals with excitement. As I perform with them over several nights that trip, I catch myself glancing up at that same moose banner hanging over the stage and I feel the joy bubbling up inside me and spilling over. I was HERE! Nothing else mattered! I honestly couldn't have cared less what actually happened onstage, I was just so damn overcome with gratitude and elation to be there. They were some of the best improv shows of my entire life.

Our first experience of a Canadian winter arrives almost overnight: one day the streets are clear and the next, we're in snow-world. While some Canadians grumble about snow's accompanying workload; shovelling footpaths, scraping windscreens, dressing up kids in five zillion layers (ok, I was with them on that one), to us, the whole thing is beyond magical.

Of course, this means the ski hills have opened... and with them, our invitation to step into the completely foreign world of snow sports.

I'd tried my hand at surfing over the years, with enough success to keep it enjoyable, but enough failure to ensure I stayed humble. I honestly couldn't call myself a surfer. But goddamn it if we were in Canada, we were gonna learn how to do cool shit in the snow!

The first time we arrive on the hill, Mt Norquay, the smallest and closest of the Bow Valley's ski mountains, I am hit by the unbelievably expensive, bulky and time-consuming amount of gear one has to contend with before you've even set amply-covered foot on the ground. It is utterly exhausting. But, I surmise, for everybody to endure it EVERY time they want to hit the slopes, it must be worth it. From what I've heard about the first time everybody tries heroin, they shit themselves and vomit and feel utterly horrendous… to even be willing to attempt to push through that crap again means the stuff must be pretty damn good. Did I really just compare snowboarding to heroin? Yes, yes, I did. Good heavens. Let's move on.

As we get ourselves sorted out, adding layer upon layer of clothes, mittens, beanies (or 'toques' as we were now calling them), helmets and goggles and socks and boots and aaaaaaaaghhhhh everything and more in the cosy warmth of the lodge, I point out the window.

'Look!' I say to my probably-not-listening family, pointing with glee at the dozens of happy bodies crissing and crossing over the fluffy ice cream snow with such effortlessness and joy it practically demands its own soundtrack. 'That's going to be us soon!'

CHAPTER 5 YOU KNOW, IF YOU WANNA STAY IN CANADA FOREVER, IT'S REAL EASY...

How soon, I wasn't sure, but, like most wonderful, longed-for achievements, they must be created on a foundation of delusion.

As I watch the snow bunnies it strikes me how wonderful it is just to see adults playing. To be using nature like a huge playground. To be enjoying something not to make money, but purely for the fun of it.

It was like little Jenny was saying 'God I've missed this!'

We don't have any money for lessons; the thrift store and garage sales have allowed us to deck ourselves out in the most economical snow get-ups known to man... and they have the 'nobody's worn this since the 80s and possibly even then it was questionable' vibe. I couldn't care less. We are warm! We are ready! Let's go!

So, thrifty as ever, we make our way up the conveyor belt and to the top of the beginners' hill, or the 'bunny hill' as it's known to us experts.

The beautiful thing about this place is that there are ALWAYS lessons for beginners in progress. With all the subtlety of a novice Aussie wearing a full-length fluoro striped snowsuit, I whisper encouraging instruction to the kids, relayed as faithfully as I can from what I eavesdrop and overhear from the instructions. 'Pizza shape!' I say. 'Do your pizza!'

Ella takes to it like a duck to water, or more accurately like a mongoose to ice. Within a couple of hours, she is confidently making the bunny hill her bunny bitch. Caleb, however, quickly makes up his mind that skiing holds about as much interest for him as reading Nietzsche. This is about a third of the way up the travelator. His 'skiing' experience consists of me supporting him from behind, holding onto his waist for balance while he ventures forward, only to give up seconds later, pulling his legs up from the snow in protest so now I'm holding his entire body weight while walking him down the hill, begging him to put down his feet, and calling out encouragingly when one of his skis occasionally scrapes the ground. Oh, and while he whinges every second about how much he hates it. As it turns out, he hates the creche only slightly less.

Tim and I are on team snowboard. Tim, an avid high school skateboarder, as predicted, picks it up quickly. I've been warned that learning to board is particularly hard. You have to accept you're likely to spend the first day on your butt, but then all of a sudden you'd have a breakthrough and BAM! You'd be doing it!

Chapter 5 You Know, If You Wanna Stay in Canada Forever, It's Real Easy...

As this prophecy comes to pass, and I find my bottom half becoming one with the snow while my top half is trying not to literally ingest it, I look up towards the heavens – aka the proper ski hill, covered in graceful gazelles floating down it like it's part of their very DNA, it is all I can do not to burst out into song as Ariel: 'I want to be where the people are, I want to see, want to see them boarding...'

If ONLY, I think, if ONLY I can get to that point where I can stand on my board and slide down that hill, then I'll be so happy, and life will be perfect.

Oh snowboarding. You and your metaphors have taught me so much.

It takes hours of eating humble snow-pie until I finally find myself able to balance enough to stay upright. Inch by inch, I edge my way down the bunny hill, until I again find enough delusional bravado to jump on the chairlift and attempt my first green (i.e. easy) hill! I can do this! I have arrived! I'm sure that there are Canadians looking at me thinking 'I cannot believe it's only her first day! I've never seen this before. She must be... *The Chosen One*!'

Minutes later I meet my nemesis... the exit of the chair lift. It will be weeks before I can actually face this enemy without falling headfirst into the ground.

But even the tiniest taste of success, however fleeting, has me hooked. Dare I say it? I am a snowboarder!

It begins to dawn on me as I progress in my snowboarding and my improv, that there are so many parallels between the two. To have any hope of succeeding, you have to be willing to risk failure. And not *if*, but *when* you fail, you have to shake it off and move on, and try to leave the fear behind. Bringing that memory with you only makes the chances of falling over again that much higher.

Just as in improv, when you're snowboarding you may have an *idea* of where you want to go. But when you're up and running, success rests on your ability to pay attention, let go of your plans, and just let it happen. Sure, you might consciously and instinctively lean your weight one way to direct things, but the mountain has a way of presenting you with bumps and powder and ice and divots and gravity and all of these unexpected surprises – not to mention other people – to navigate as they happen. You can't pre-plan. Or you can, but you've gotta be willing to abandon the plan at any given second and deal with what's happening now.

If I'm incredibly calm and confident on my board, I'm amazed by how fast I can actually go. It's incredible. But the second I think, 'Oh shit, I can't do this!', BAM! I lose my footing and take a solid tumble. Being in my own head is a shortcut to failure.

Comedy wise, aside from Loose Moose and chipping away at my video store education, I'm doing relatively little stand up. It's time. I score a five-minute opening spot at Yuk Yuks, Calgary's main comedy club and part of the biggest chain in Canada. I am stoked. When I'm making the hour and a half trek from Canmore to Calgary, it starts snowing. 'I've got this,' I think. 'I've driven in snow before.' But soon, the blizzard is so bad that I can't even see the lines on the road... Trucks are passing me on either side and spraying my windscreen with black icy sludge. I try to breathe away my panic and push on, resolute that it is my first shot at stand-up in Canada and I cannot let my professionalism be called into question on day ONE! But then a little voice says to me, 'You know, if you get killed for a five-minute comedy spot, I WILL BE SO PISSED AT YOU!'

I miss the gig.

Spoiler: I'm still alive.

I get other spots at Yuk Yuk's, and it's after one of these that they offer me my first ever mini-comedy tour. It will be four days on the road supporting a headliner, performing each night at various venues throughout British Columbia. This is how they do it; they run lots of satellite gigs all over Canada, sending out two comics at a time, one support doing 30 minutes, the headliner doing an hour, both sharing the driving to cut down on expenses.

The day of the tour arrives – and more specifically, my headliner arrives at my doorstep at 7 in the morning for us to commence our adventure.

I have no idea what to expect: I don't know this guy from a bar of Rocky Mountain soap (incidentally, a beautiful local product made right here in Canmore), all I know is that we'll be squeezed into a car for the next nine hours and then some, meaning that despite my excitement, there is absolutely real potential for an extremely awkward few days.

His name is Dan Rock. I open the door and there he is: a thirty-something clean cut guy wearing jeans, a baseball cap and on either side of his neck, a tattoo of the holes in the side of a violin. He is an American stand-up comedian who apparently comes up to Canada every year to do the Canadian circuit. He's been doing stand-up professionally for well over a decade and now teaches it as well, and to my utter relief and delight, we not only hit it off like a house on fire but spend the ensuing days in what feels like a one-on-one masterclass. All while driving through the most

Chapter 5   You Know, If You Wanna Stay in Canada Forever, It's Real Easy...

stunning views of snow-covered British Columbia, with jaw-dropping sights of mountains and lakes at every turn. It is so endlessly beautiful it is almost too much, like you are overdosing on a visual buffet and will soon pass out. The biggest thing Dan teaches me during this trip is to care less onstage. Not care less about comedy, definitely not care less about the audience, but about myself.

'Don't worry about sticking to your script,' he says. 'You especially, you're an improviser! Let go! Just see what happens! If you're inspired to go with something, just go for it.'

That night, we arrive at the most stunning, quaint, Swiss-style adorable ski resort I've ever seen to this day.

Imagine the sweetest little Euro-style village, filled with A frame chalets, old fashioned lamp posts, with fairy lights everywhere reflecting off the fresh scrumptious snow, and you have Sunpeaks Ski Resort.

My heart is bursting. My room for the night is five star and it feels like I've won some kind of lottery. A few short years ago I'd set foot on stage not even knowing how to plug in my guitar. Now THIS is possible? What the heck?!

The gig itself is in the downstairs bar; it is poorly attended but the crowd is friendly. Possibly fuelled by the high of just being there, on tour in these soul-lifting surrounds, I throw caution to the blizzard and take Dan's advice, abandon my set list and improvise, playing with the crowd. At one point I leap offstage to hug a latecomer. The gig, to my delighted surprise, is awesome. I learn that the most important thing of all is your connection with the crowd. Sometimes sticking stubbornly to the script can DISCONNECT you. Acknowledging the truth of the environment and treating the audience like new friends with whom you want to hang out and have a great time is my thing. I don't realise it at the time, but this magical experience is transforming me. I am beginning to find my voice.

The next morning I'm dressed in my so-dreadful-it's-awesome snowsuit and meet up with the MC from the gig at the chairlift, who's invited me for a morning of boarding together. He works at Sunpeaks full time running events and is to this day one of the most memorable characters I've ever met. The night before he'd been dressed in top-to-toe Rastafarian clothes, which I thought was a gimmick for the comedy night. But the next morning, here he is, dressed from top to toe in Rastafarian snow gear. Snow pants, snow jacket, snowboard, helmet… it is as if Bob Marley has taken up residence at the North Pole.

Chapter 5   You Know, If You Wanna Stay in Canada Forever, It's Real Easy...

'Jenny!' he greets me cheerfully. 'Are you pumped and ready to do our five-mile Green Run?'

'You betchya!' I reply, genuinely thrilled.

On the way up on the chair lift, he pulls a beer can out of his jacket, pops it open and hands it to me. It's 10am.

'Fuck it,' I think. 'When in Sunpeaks...'

Once we finish the beer, he pulls out a massive joint, lights it and hands it to me. It is 10.13am.

'Fuck it,' I think. 'I'm childfree, I haven't smoked in years, I had the gig of my life last night and I'm on tour and this is turning out to be FUCKING AWESOME!'

As we near the top of the ski lift, it occurs to me that the farthest I've ever snowboarded in one hit is around 500m on an easy hill. Now here I am about to board not even double that, but EIGHT FREAKING KILOMETRES. After having had a beer and half a joint for breakfast. I am both terrified and delighted. Comedy truly is the new rock'n'roll.

There is so much beautiful soft snow everywhere that through my admittedly very high eyes I would swear the trees have been squirted from top to bottom with fresh whipped cream, and that we are in fact, boarding down a mountain made of ice-cream in a dessert buffet. Ah, ice-cream. Did I mention I am stoned?

Bob Marley is giving me a private tutorial the whole way down, and while my legs soon become jelly, we all know what jelly goes well with: ice-cream! It is divine. By the time we get to the bottom some hours later, I feel like I am a different snowboarder. I can turn properly; I trust myself to go harder and faster than I'd ever thought was possible: I feel like I'm a pro. To this day, that bizarre morning still ranks as one of the most magical of my life.

Somewhere amidst the snowboarding and the hiking and the biking, we decide to embark on another impulsive adventure: having another baby. Our little man Cassidy is born on a very snowy night and immediately proves himself to be incredibly Canadian. He is outrageously sweet and ridiculously accommodating from day one.

His calm and easy nature means that we can still come to shows at the Moose with little stress; he just chills and sleeps throughout. He comes onstage with me when he is three weeks old in an improvised scene that I decide could use an incredibly cute baby.

Chapter 5 You Know, If You Wanna Stay in Canada Forever, It's Real Easy...

By this point we move from our gorgeous ski-town to a place about an hour on the other side of Calgary, called High River. It has a charm of its own, but compared to the outdoorsy snow wonderland of Canmore, in wintertime it is a ghost town. Everybody stays indoors. This, combined with having a newborn in the household and being new to this area, makes things feel very, very lonely.

We are coming up to our two-year anniversary in Canada. We have the Permanent Residency paperwork in hand and intend to use it. But when push comes to shove, we just can't. Plus, a timely convergence of complications makes us feel like a return to Oz is all but written in the stars. Ella, now nearly seven, is increasingly homesick, literally crying every week for her auntie Ang. Tim's school is unwilling to renew his teaching contract until they've confirmed the next year's enrolment numbers. Plus, we are gradually realising that staying in Canada will mean we won't be seeing our Aussie family more than a few times in our kids' childhoods (curse you, expensive transPacific flights!).

We make the call. We're moving back to Australia.

A few days before we leave, I perform a work-in-progress version of my first full length solo show at Loose Moose. It's the one I developed during a residency at the Banff Centre for the Arts and would eventually evolve into '*An*

Unexpected Variety Show', my comedy cabaret that I would tour in Australia and beyond.

On opening night, I sit panicked and frazzled backstage, with the kids milling about behind the curtain. Cassidy is attached to my boob as I madly try to apply some semblance of stage makeup in the dark with whatever I can find in my friend's handbag. (I've just discovered I've overlooked bringing my own, neither the first nor the last time, I must admit). It is a fringe festival show with super strict regulations on timing, and as such, when the clock strikes 7, the curtains open NO MATTER WHAT.

I all but pull Cassidy's suction off like a plunger off an uncooperative sink, hand the kids over to my friend who has kindly volunteered to babysit in the games room, and the show begins. Despite all I've learned at the Moose over the past two years, I feel anything BUT relaxed and playful and charming. But I settle in, give it my best shot and at the end of the show, in which I sit and sing a 'duet' with an old cassette recording of my real Mum, I think I hear somebody in the audience dealing with a bad cold. As the lights go up and I take my bow, I can see that some people are crying. A woman hugs me on the way out.

'You know her?' asks Dennis.

Chapter 5   You Know, If You Wanna Stay in Canada Forever, It's Real Easy...

'No,' I say.

The show is sooooo far from perfect it's not funny, but, based on its reaction on this first incredibly raw night, I'm sure there's something there. Tim gives me a huge hug afterwards and says, 'I think this is only the beginning.'

The following night he stays home with the kids while Mama hits the stage. On the final night I get my first ever standing ovation. I am literally moved to tears. I drive home completely buzzing… to find all three kids screaming their heads off and that my son has gastro.

Ah showbiz. You crazy minx.

Chapter 6 Car Crashes And Caboolture

hat's the difference between a head on collision and Caboolture?

Nothing. They're both a car wreck. And you'll be lucky to get out of either of them alive.

We all have umpteen examples in our own lives to prove that things rarely, if ever, go according to plan. I've had plenty already, but the latest glaring one is spending nearly half a decade living somewhere I never could have imagined. From my childhood (childish?) dreams of living large in New York City, or Berlin, or even Kathmandu, I never for a moment thought that I could, or would, spend a significant chunk of my life living in… da da da DA… Caboolture.

For those of you not familiar with this little pocket of the world, know that it's about an hour north of Brisbane, and known as one of 'those' places. Lower socio-economic demographic, a 'bogan casserole', if you will.

Even the mention of it is enough to get a laugh onstage. Oh yes, in my comedy world, living there is a veritable – in a low-hanging fruit kinda way – goldmine of material. But living there feels like one massive earthly lesson in trying very, very hard not to be judgemental.

And failing dismally.

I try, really, I do. But the sights of pregnant teenagers yelling at their toddlers in K-Mart (making me wonder what the hell goes on behind closed doors, given that our best parenting – presumably – comes out on public display), to seeing kids barely potty-trained but excelling in potty-mouth, to my kids coming into the kitchen reporting that they've just heard the lady up the road's small child is in hospital after being beaten by her partner… I can't help it. I try not to overthink it, to remember that 'bogans are people too', (I even wrote a song to that effect, it's going to be my

Chapter 6   Car Crashes And Caboolture

'We Are the World') but I can't help it. Living in Caboolture really gets me down.

But… it's undeniably the most practical option for us right now. Tim has gotten a teaching job here. And it's cheap as chips, I'll give it that.

We live in a modern – as in, brand freaking new – four bedroom house with a double garage and sizeable yard for the price of a 1-bedroom unit in Brisbane. It makes life simple; I'll give it that too. Less than five minutes' drive to get pretty much anywhere to keep life ticking over. But that's the thing: it feels to me like that's all we are doing: keeping life ticking over.

A few weeks after we move, three things happen in rapid succession: I am injured in a head-on car accident, my baby boy – all fifteen months of him – starts day-care and on his very first day falls off a piece of equipment and breaks his leg, and my six year old gets an Evil Dead level stomach virus. The three of us are in a queue at the chemist waiting for our combined cocktail of medicinal aids when Mister 6 looks at me, pale and pleading the way any human is when they're about to vomit and they're desperately hoping you can do something to make it not so. I shake my head at him, pleading with him no. He eyeballs me back, assuring me yes. This is going to happen.

I swear I grab him by the scruff of his neck and all but lift him through the air to the open area outside Woolworths where I spy a nearby bin. I pull him towards it just in the nick of time and he unleashes projectile hell. As my stomach turns just listening to him, I suddenly feel the urge to laugh. What we must look like. Me with a full neck brace barely able to move, holding my baby on my hip with his full-length leg cast, pushing my son's head into a public bin so he can empty his guts. I feel like screaming, 'Caboolture, there's a new sheriff in town! YIPPEE KAY AYE MOTHERFUCKERS.'

A little rainbow in the middle of this shitstorm presents itself in the most unexpected way at the magical wonderland that is the annual Woodford Folk Festival. It's like a mini-Glastonbury meets Woodstock with more chai.

I perform there regularly, you see, and love every moment onstage. It's my kind of audience. This year as I'm performing, my littlest is crawling around the sandpit at the kids' festival and seems to quickly build a budding baby bond of friendship with two adorable twins around the same age. Their mother, a tall stunning blonde with long hair all the way down her back is nearby and we get chatting, quickly hitting it off like a house on fire. Now I NEVER swap numbers with strangers. Not because I'm aloof, but rather because I have enough friendships in my

Chapter 6 Car Crashes And Caboolture

life that I can barely service, let alone adding more people that I can disappoint and neglect.

But I adore this woman immediately; her name is Hatty and it's friendship love at first sight. We find ourselves swapping contact details and walking away into the sunset with promises of playdates floating on the balmy festival breeze.

A couple of nights later, she and I bump into each other again, but this time I'm all sequins and make-up, on my way backstage.

'Look at you!' she says. 'What are you all glammed up for?'

'I'm performing tonight! You should come!'

'Oh! I didn't know you were a performer!' she says.

'Yeah, I'm a comedian.'

'Are you really?' she says. 'Wow! You know, I went to school back in England with a comedian, I don't know if you've heard of him…'

INSERT DRAMATIC PAUSE.

'… Bill Bailey?'

I do believe the entire Woodford Folk Festival site felt a tremor measuring at least 8.4, this being my jaw hitting the organic chai-infused earth.

You see, not only have I heard of Bill Bailey but I'm not exaggerating even one iota when I say that HE IS MY FAVOURITE COMEDIAN IN THE ENTIRE UNIVERSE. Nobody in comedy, living or dead, has influenced my comedy more than him. The first time I saw 'Part Troll,' my life changed. Truly.

When I first watch it, I'm just starting to build a small profile in the Brissie comedy scene and we're just about to make the leap to Canada, i.e. I already have huge dreams aplenty! But when I see this show, it's like a beautiful performing nymph taps me on the shoulder and whispers 'Aha! This! THIS! This is what you want to do!'

Once I've semi-recovered from my shock, she goes on to tell me that they've known each other since they were teenagers, that he used to play funny songs for entertainment at parties – including her own 18th! – and that whenever he tours Australia they catch up.

Chapter 6 Car Crashes And Caboolture

Cut to a couple of months and several playdates later, when Hatty sends me a text: 'Bill is coming in July!'

A small part of me floats off to a higher realm, and to be honest, I'm not quite sure if it's ever returned.

In July 2010, I'm dressed up and psyching up to tick a previously seemingly untickable box off my bucket list: to see Bill Bailey live AND meet him afterwards.

This show is amazing, as expected. He does about fifteen thousand encores, half of which happen as a genuine surprise once most of the crowd has left the building. I love that so much, as do the remaining audience members, just knowing that he doesn't have to come back out but does so because he wants to.

And then, once all is said and done, it's time to head backstage.

Now as much as I am over the moon about meeting my comedic mentor/inspiration number one, I've also spent much of the past week trying to psyche myself down for it. That is, not to get my hopes up too high and prepare for the reality that our introduction will in all likelihood consist of 'Nice to meet you! Well I'm really exhausted and off to the hotel now.'

We walk into the dressing room; a daunting sight for Bill, I'm sure, with his childhood friend, followed by five other adoring women descending on his backstage refuge like some sort of comedy industry harem.

To my utter delight, Bill is ridiculously, genuinely, friendly and super hospitable, offering us his wine, nibblies, beers, whatever happens to be in the room short of the mirrors and fixtures.

The whole time I'm trying to hold my shizz together and not devolve into a slobbering mess such that security will kick me out for not having the required minimum grasp on reality.

I gulp.

'I'm a comedian too, I do musical comedy and I don't want to be all gushy, but you've really inspired me so much…'

All the women in the room say 'awwww.' It makes me feel supported and also a bit like I'm on some sort of bizarre comedic dating show.

We talk about whether I would ever do the Edinburgh Festival, the logistics of which kinda hurt my head, what with having a small family in tow.

Chapter 6 Car Crashes And Caboolture

'Well,' Bill says, 'I'd certainly be very happy to do what I can to help you out.'

AAAGH![4]

I cannot believe this moment happens.

I'm tempted to ring Mum and let her know, but I know that her genuine pride mixed with elderly confusion will mean she'll soon be telling everybody who'll listen that the lovely Gandalf man from Lord of the Philosopher's Stone has decided to retire and hand over his entire career to me.

To add to this joy-nugget of an evening, a bizarre turn of events leads to me finding myself driving him back from the Sunshine Coast to Brisbane – one on one with my hero for two hours – which we spend geeking out about comedy together.

Even living in Caboolture, magic bloody well happens.

---

[4] At the time of writing, I have yet to take him up on that offer, but still. AAAAGH!

On the downside, the crash back to reality of life in the 'Booltch is a little more violent than usual.

I am thoroughly committed to actively hating my life.

One day we achieve that winning combination of being out of petrol AND having zero bucks in the bank until payday, X days away. Thus, in a beautiful moment that will doubtless be part of my memoir one day (SPOILER) I resort to using the tin opener to cut open my daughter's piggy bank, shamefully count up all the coins within and head on down to the petrol station to put exactly eight dollars and thirty five cents worth of unleaded into the tank.

As I walk up to the service counter, there's a woman covered in tattoos and with straggly hair standing by the packets of chips, barking ineffectual orders at several small children who are running amok. I hate my life.

I approach the customer service lady, tip my handfuls of coins onto the counter and start counting them out, only to have her interrupt me: 'I'm not legally obliged to accept that.'

'I'm sorry, what?'

Chapter 6   Car Crashes And Caboolture

'All those coins,' she says, gesturing with a combo of judgement and little enthusiasm, 'I'm not legally obliged to accept THIS many coins.'

I stare at her for a second. I consider saying, 'Are you fucking kidding me?' but instead just put my head down and keep counting, hoping against hope that she'll reconsider her legal stance if I just press on as planned: as it turns out I'm ten cents short anyway.

FARK.

Suddenly from behind me, a hand slaps down on the counter a ten dollar note. I turn around. It's the mum. The one dripping with toddlers, tattoos and my judgement. She smiles at me. 'There, it's yours.'

I'm gobsmacked and to be honest, pretty embarrassed.

'No, I couldn't…'

'No, go on,' she says. 'You need it more than me.'

In that moment, the moment I will forever reflect on as being saved by 'the girl with the full-sleeve tattoos', I realise I am a deeply shitty person.

Why the hell do I think I'm any better than any other person living in Caboolture? I'm not. I'm a judgey piece of shit.

I try to pull up my socks and make the most of it.

A year or so into our Caboolturean cultural immersion, fortune strikes. I get a ridiculously lucrative one-off gig, part of the proceeds of which allow me to attend an improv masterclass in upstate New York. It's in the Catskills. The only thing I know about this was that it is where Baby met Johnny at Kellerman's so she could be de-babied and have the time of her life dirty dancing.

The retreat centre itself does not actually look too dissimilar from the resort in the movie, though instead of spending weeks of being lifted towards heaven by Patrick Swayze, dealing with illegal abortions and carrying watermelons, I improvise my butt off. I am working with and learning from some incredible people who will become my friends for life.

Including Gary Austin.

Gary is most notably known for co-founding the famous Groundlings Theatre in LA, a comedy institution whose alumni include Will Ferrell, Lisa Kudrow, Kristen Wiig,

Chapter 6   Car Crashes And Caboolture

Melissa McCarthy and plenty more. Helen Hunt thanked him in her Oscar speech.

In person, I find him both intimidating and adorable. I am drawn to him but too starstruck to even say hello.

One night, after a student show, I see him sitting in a rare moment alone. Figuring it's now or never, I muster up the guts to approach him.

'Hi!' I say.

'Hi!' he says.

We chat casually – meaning I nervously make small talk and try to sound intelligent – until he says to me: 'You know, you are really good. You need to come to LA and work with me.'

BOOM.

The seed is planted.

A year later, thanks to a grant from the Ian Potter Cultural Trust, I am indeed in LA, working with Gary on solo improvisation and… my solo show. The one I'd first drafted at the Banff Centre many moons ago and debuted in its draft form at Loose Moose Theatre.

Gary wants to direct it.

FARK.

I perform it in his loungeroom to an audience of just him. Well, him and his two beloved dogs.

It's terrifying. I would feel a zillion times more comfortable performing this in front of hundreds of strangers.

He listens and watches, saying nothing. I finish. He takes a moment, looks thoughtful, then stands up. 'You know, this is very exciting what you're doing.' We begin.

A year later, I'm debuting the show for its first full festival season at Melbourne Fringe. I've brought my littlest – all two years of him – with me. We're staying with my super generous family friends, so at least rent isn't an issue, or at least not in terms of accommodation…

I'm not sure many 'civilians' realise the financial realities that performers face. Yes, sure I'll bet they get the whole 'showbiz is unstable' thing, but whenever I tell somebody that I'm performing in a festival, their impressed reaction makes me think they must believe I'm getting paid. The reality is that when a performer is doing a festival, not only are they usually not getting paid, the artist themselves IS PAYING to perform.[5]

Venue hire. Sound and lighting tech people. Promotion and marketing. Flyers and posters. Festival registration fees, which are usually hundreds of dollars and allow you the privilege of being included in their program and website and having the cachet of their logo on your promo material, all of which again, THE ARTIST PAYS FOR, regardless of ticket sales – or lack of them.

See what I mean about doing comedy feeling akin to a gambling problem?

But the show *is* good. I know it's good. Gary Freaking Austin has given me his tough love rewriting/digging deep/one-on-one wisdom that has completely transformed my rough sketch of a show into something that feels like it really is the best of me.

---

[5] Some curated festivals do pay you outright. But when you're doing a run of your show at most festivals – i.e. you're the one producing it – this usually means you're the one who's putting their money on the line.

I have to back myself.

This festival being in Melbourne of course, means paying for flights, plus finding a babysitter for show-times. Even on a shoestring, my budget has blown out to a few thousand dollars.

Gulp.

But I have to back myself, right?

I invite every person I can think of – including some I barely know – to opening night. I figure if I can pack it out and it goes well, then word of mouth will spread, the rest of the season will sell well and Mama's roulette wheel will come up on black, rather than deep in the red.

Opening night, I'm a wreck.

My littlest has NOT been happy with me leaving, completely understandable given he's in a new place with a new babysitter while Mummy's stressedly distracted by her new baby: her show.

Frazzled and freezing – like many venues, the theatre, while stunning, is not heated backstage – I try to warm up, temperature wise and vocally.

Chapter 6   Car Crashes And Caboolture

I peek out from behind the curtain and watch the audience trickle in. I smile with excitement and love, seeing some of my beautiful friends I haven't seen in ages take their seats. Then I spot somebody and my heart squeals: Tim Bloody Ferguson.

I am first exposed to the comedy of Tim in the Doug Anthony Allstars, while at uni, when two of my closest friends religiously put DAAS videos on repeat while we drink cheap wine and eat noodles.

A few months before this opening night, I attend a comedy writing workshop taught by Tim. When I mention what I do, he says 'Wow! A musical comedian, eh?'

I'm not sure what he means by this, but I somehow feel enough of a connection and confidence in at least his friendliness, that I email him and invite him to my Melbourne show.

And HOLY SHIT HE'S TURNED UP.

I feel over the moon already and I haven't even set a foot onstage. That's a feeling, or perhaps rather an attitude, that I still try to cultivate to this day. That rather than freak myself out with thoughts of 'How will this go? Will I be any good? Will they like me?' (by the way, all of which are only nerve-inducing and incredibly narcissistic) I try to remember what a privilege it is just to be onstage. To perform in front of actual people on an actual stage with as much joy as I had performing in front of Mum from the stage of her bedroom. I want to always remember the JOY in performing.

The show goes smoothly and afterwards I am thrilled beyond thrilled when Tim joins me and my friends at our table in the bar and chats with us for well over an hour. Is there nothing better than discovering that people you hugely admire from afar are, in fact, wonderful human beings in real life?

Since then, Tim Ferguson has continued to be a brilliant supporter of my work; that night, I feel that no matter WHAT happens for the rest of this festival run, I am happy.

It is like I've laid down a challenge for the theatre gods.

My Oprah-like gratitude is stretched beyond its limits. I refuse to look at my ticket sales before each show; it makes me too nervous and besides, what does it matter? Whether it's ten people or a hundred, they still deserve the same energy and effort from me.

Chapter 6 Car Crashes And Caboolture

So night after night, I get my toddler ready, say a very tearful goodbye – sometimes with him screaming for me not to leave – walk across a football field, catch two trams to the theatre, set up my stage and props, go to my cold dressing room to warm up, then emerge from the curtains to start the show, which begins in blackness. As the lights fade up during the opening number, I look out into the audience of my 120-seat theatre. Night after night, it's a similar shock. Two people. Three people. One night there are seven. And they are ALL THEATRE STAFF. They feel sorry for me having sold zero tickets so are providing the bodies so that the show may go on. They give me a standing ovation at the end. I take a photo of it. I love them.

But each night it's the same. A beautiful and appreciative crowd… that also happens to be miniscule. I do what I always try to do with a challenging gig: amuse myself with the absurdity of it and tell myself 'Oh, well, it's one for the memoirs!'[6]

But afterwards I trudge out of the theatre, take two trams and a freezing walk across the football field home, pay my babysitter more money than I've made in days, snuggle up with my beautiful sleeping little boy and cry.

---

[6] And whaddya know? In this case I was right!

By the time the festival is nearly over, I feel broken.

I ring my husband, back home in Queensland, bawling my eyes out. 'What have I done?' I sob down the line, referring to the nearly three thousand dollars I am in the red. 'I've completely fucked us.'

I jump online and enrol in a Graduate Diploma of Education. A teacher. I'll be a teacher. Drama. It'll be fun. I can inspire the next generation of wannabe performers to follow their fruitless dreams before they too move into the far more sensible role of teaching the next generation of wannabe performers.

It's the third last night of the festival. I'm exhausted and also relieved: the end is in sight. Of the festival, and possibly also my career. But I can hold my head high. I've tried. I haven't won, but I've tried.

After my show, a couple of the theatre staff – with whom, after my personal show for their pleasure, I've become quite bonded – invite me to jump in a cab to head to the Fringe Hub for the festival awards party. I hesitate, thinking a warm doona under which I can bury my self-pity is in my near future, but then think 'Fuck it. This has been a bloody marathon. It's time to have a night off!'

Chapter 6 Car Crashes And Caboolture

We arrive to a hall heaving with hundreds of artists, creatives and other groovy people of Melbourne. I'm squished in right near the back, all but gulping down my second bourbon when I hear 'Excellence in Cabaret: The Unexpected Variety Hour!' I freeze. That's not quite the title of my show, but near enough. (It's 'Show', not 'Hour.') But… surely there can't be another show called nearly the same thing? Had I won? WTF? Nobody had even come to see it. How could this be? What?

I look at my friends Tess Waters and Kai Smythe who are nodding excitedly at me. 'Yes! It's you! Go!'

I run through the crowd, trying to part the seas like a mad fringe festival Moses. When I finally make it near the stage, I realise I'm still carrying my quite large handbag, so unceremoniously dump it right in the middle of the crowd and climb onstage. I'm almost hyperventilating in disbelief. I hold up the award, giggling, to mad cheers from the audience, who I know full well have no idea who I am. It is sheer unadulterated magic.

Backstage, among the other award winners, all high on their wins and downing the free sparkling wine on offer, I call Tim. We laugh and squeal and I set a record for the number of times saying 'I can't believe it' in a row, like a broken Cricket the Talking Doll.

FUNNY MUMMY

The last two nights I have an actual audience, thanks to news of the award. It doesn't sell out, but it's close enough to make me feel like a happy ending to this rollercoaster.

On my final night, my wonderful hosts surprise me with an unbelievable tiramisu from Brunetti's (the most fabulous patisserie in Melbourne) and champagne, while my beautiful theatre crew give me flowers and a show poster with their well wishes scrawled all over it.

When it's all done, I catch my two trams, walk across the football field, pay my babysitter more money than I've made from the whole festival, climb into bed with my beautiful boy and cry. Again.

Then I sit bolt upright, grab my computer, log in and cancel my uni enrolment.

It's back to reality again.

Tim and I try to keep the flame alive through date nights. It all sounds good, but somehow, we always end up in the food court at the shopping centre in Morayfield, polish off an almost so unromantic the-comedy-writes-itself meal of a kebab, sit in the $2 massage chairs and try to think of things

Chapter 6 Car Crashes And Caboolture

to say to one another. I am obsessed with comedy. He is obsessed with Christianity. We are destined to spend our days embarrassing the shit out of each other. He is all 'Oh: My God!' while I am burying my head in my hands, all 'Oh. My. God.'

In other words, it's gonna be a bloody long life together.

In early 2013, I find a lump in my breast. Despite my own irritation at my tendency to over-dramatise every possible occurrence in my life, I freak out just enough to re-evaluate my life. What if the news turns out to be the worst? What if I only have one or two years left? I know that's me just getting ahead of myself and that in all likelihood it's going to be fine, but still, it's like a lightning bolt has struck and is pulling everything into focus. Life **is** finite. How have I forgotten this? And now that I've been reminded, what do I actually want to do with the life I have left?

To my surprise, the first thoughts are not of things like 'I must make sure I perform that comedy show I've been dreaming of' or 'I have to travel the whole world!' But rather, 'I need to get the hell out of Caboolture.' It really is like a lightning bolt.

I am in the wrong place. If I'm going to die, my hugest regret will be not spending my life in a place that I love. In a place that inspires me. In a place where I belong.

The lump, thank heavens, is benign. But with the sigh of relief comes another sigh; one of longing for the life I've been envisioning should I only have a little bit of time left. This non-event has made me re-evaluate my life big-time and I know one thing is for sure: I need to leave.

But my husband and kids seem happy here. Don't they? I have reservations about their school not being up to the standard that I would prefer; not that it's not okay; it is, generally, but academically and extra-curricular wise, I worry that they are sacrificing the quality of the education for the devoutness of the Christianity. Even my husband, an incredibly committed Christian, finds some of the 'education' a little too hardcore, i.e. when their 'science class' talks seriously about the first six days of creation.

Riiiiiiggghhhhhhht.

Let me repeat. They learned this in *science class*.

But anyway, the kids are settled here. And my husband, while not really challenged in any way, is at least very comfortable in his job as a Distance Education Teacher.

Chapter 6 Car Crashes And Caboolture

Caboolture is cheap. The kids are content. My husband is satisfied. Am I the real problem? Can't I just suck it up and be happy?

My marriage of 11 years isn't working. I tell myself that the reason it isn't working is because of our surrounds.

We can never be happy together because I am desperately unhappy *here*.

One evening in late 2013, after managing to get some long overdue babysitting, my husband accompanies me to a comedy gig. It is a corporate function, MCing the launch of an arts program in the Moreton Bay Region and, as with all corporate gigs, where the audience has literally invested nothing in seeing you onstage, I am not expecting too much. However, I am pleasantly surprised – it goes beautifully. Afterwards, as we load my keyboard into the car, my husband turns to me and says 'I forgot how magical you are onstage. You need to pursue this. I know there are plenty of reasons to stay here but I think if you don't really go for it, you're always going to regret it.' I'll owe him forever for that.

Within a month, we are in Melbourne.

Chapter 7 The Year My Life Broke

Our dream life is finally here. After tossing up where precisely to live in Melbourne – and being slapped in the face with the realisation that our rent has tripled, and our backyard has disappeared – we finally choose to go with the option we feel will bring the best of both worlds. The Dandenongs.

Close enough to Melbourne to still actively pursue the more plentiful opportunities in the comedy world but set in a magical Enid Blyton-esque forest. It's filled with charming little buildings, and coils of smoke from log fires twist through the air that make the town smell like a wood fire. It is everything Caboolture isn't. It's character-full, rather than characters-full, though it has that going for it too. Instead of screaming young mothers, it has socially progressive creatives. And even its own wizard. Seriously, they have their own wizard; but I digress. The Dandenongs are quaint, unique and, above all, completely and deliciously inspiring.

We are all besotted.

It feels like we've won the lottery. We've found the most beautiful dream-like three level practically-a-treehouse to rent, on acreage no less. We buy our long-dreamed about Labrador and call him Bublé (yes, as in Michael Bublé). I can tell instantly if somebody is on my wavelength based on their reaction when they hear his name. If they laugh, *welcome into my sacred world of silliness, friend!* I'm not adverse to Michael Bublé, but neither am I a huge fan. I've just always thought Bublé would make a hilarious dog name – and indeed, it does. Aside from what the neighbours, passers-by and dog park goers must think when they hear us calling out 'Boobs! BOOBS! Come here Boobs!'

Chapter 7 The Year My Life Broke

We get chooks. We enrol the kids in the most stunning school, backed by a gorgeous forest. It feels like every dream we've ever had for our family life has been realised.

And yet...

Something still isn't right with our marriage. But...

'Never give up, never give up, never give up.' Winston Churchill (a man who stayed married and also committed to a drinking problem his entire life).

The wheels did start coming off quite early in our relationship.

Flashback... We are only a couple of years into our marriage, Tim is a full-time student, we are full-time broke and raising two extremely full-time young children. We are struggling in every area.

But I do not think leaving is the answer. I tell myself we just need to talk it out, and organise more date nights.

When these text-book band-aid attempts still fail, we agree that our mutual dissatisfaction is just circumstantial.

We'll suck it up and hang in there. At least until Tim is finished with uni; at least until the financial pressure is relieved; at least until the kids move naturally into a less stressful life stage.

We keep it up for another year. Then one more year. And one more year. And one more year… until we find ourselves twelve years into a marriage of two very different minds, living in Melbourne and marvelling with despair at why our new dream life still isn't cutting it.

But regardless, Tim remains resolute that divorce is not an option for the simple reason that God hates it.

Oh yes. Did I mention he is devoutly Christian? I did, right? Well let me mention it again.

The thing about being a non-Christian married to a devout Christian is… well, everything.

You're the muggle of their world, trying to be good natured and open and respectful of everyone's right to believe what they want, while also feeling embarrassed and fraudulent when other church goers assume you're on Team Potter, and unsure of whether to just let his (firm) beliefs trump your (unfirm) beliefs when it comes to the running of the family and what to tell the kids.

Chapter 7 The Year My Life Broke

And, it also means that if we do get divorced, that call will be mine and mine alone. The weight of that nearly strangles me. If I leave, it is MY fault. MY choice. MY consequences.

Doesn't it matter to him that we are not working?

'That's every marriage,' he shrugs. 'Same shit, different tinsel.'

I try to believe that, to resign myself to it. Any hope I have for more, I tell myself, is just an unrealistic fantasy. Divorce destroys kids, doesn't it? And in this case, I and I alone will be the destroyer. I don't want that.

I cannot bring myself to do it. Can't I just wait it out until the kids have left home? I also dread the thought of spending the rest of my life alone. I mean, who the heck would want to take on me and my baggage?

Most of all though, I don't want the shame of walking away. Tim is, for all intents and purposes, a nice guy. He's gentle. He's kind. He will never hurt me. Well, not in the traditional ways that spring to mind. I know he'll never cheat, thanks to the golden combo of his loyal nature and his Christian beliefs. He rarely raises his voice.

But I realise much, much later, that he does hurt me. Over and over. And I know I hurt him.

I do not wish to throw him under the bus here when he cannot defend himself. But I will say that I realise now I had bought into the idea that so many women do. That I was 'lucky' that he would 'let me' work. He would 'let me' go to perform gigs, go to work at festivals and on cruises while he stayed home with the kids, even though most of the time me working away involved me either taking kids with me and/or hiring a nanny/housekeeper and freezing meals in advance.

I come home and the kids are alive, but the house is a catastrophe. But I can't hope for more. I'm lucky. And this is my penance. My cross to bear. MY choice. MY consequences, right?

While I don't want to admit it, the effects of me being away on the kids are beginning to show. They are unsettled, ratty and anxious. But I am adamant to parent the way we planned when the kids were just an idea and not a reality: that we will be equal. Fifty-fifty. We are both equally responsible and equally capable and equally valuable and able to rear our children just as well as each other and to imply otherwise is an insult to us both. These are our ideals. When family members raise concerns about my absences

Chapter 7 The Year My Life Broke

having a negative impact on the kids, I am offended both on behalf of Tim and myself. How dare they insinuate that he isn't just as much a father as I am a mother! How dare they!

But as the years roll by, it dawns on me that ideals are wonderful and worthy and noble and should be strived towards… they're just not always compatible with reality.

Sure, both parents SHOULD be equally capable of taking care of their kids, such that it doesn't matter which parent is doing the primary caregiving (once you get past those early, lactating years, at least). But sometimes it does matter. Like when one parent struggles so much to cope with the daily grind of their own life that they just don't have enough left over to do parenting in any consistent way. No boundaries. No discipline. No effort other than that required to keep the kids from dying.

You can strive for all the equality you want, but the fallout from reality can be immense.

I stay. And I stay. And I stay.

I am so worried about disappointing Mum, who is old-fashioned and always says how happy she is that my sister and I are in stable relationships, that I tell myself I can never leave my marriage until she dies. One day I can't keep it in anymore.

'Mum,' I say. 'I know you love that I'm married, but I have to tell you, honestly, I'm finding it incredibly hard.'

'Oh Jen!' she says, grabbing my hand. 'I know! I'm not blind. I see what's happening. You know,' she leans in, almost conspiratorially, 'you only get one life.' I feel a weight lift.

We have tried so hard. We have moved to our magical life in the beautiful Dandenongs. This should be working. Once the initial buzz wears off, it becomes clearer and clearer and clearer; the problem isn't Caboolture, or financial stress, or kids. It's us. Our problems aren't situational, they're terminal. If we can't make it work here in our dream scenario, we can't make it work anywhere, or anyhow.

One day I kneel on the floor crying, scrubbing what could well have been week-old cornflakes out of the carpet yet again, and the words spill out of my mouth seemingly unbidden. It is a surprise to hear them out loud: 'I would rather be alone.' There it is.

Chapter 7 The Year My Life Broke

We tell the kids. We continue living under the same roof and realise, sadly, how markedly un-different it feels from the last few years. A month later, he moves out.

The first night after he leaves, I find myself staring at the post-dinner mess on the kitchen bench and feeling paralysed with panic. Oh my God. It's all up to me now.

Nobody else to tag team to get the kids to bed. Nobody else to take over for five minutes when you need to catch your breath. Nobody to nod along in exasperation when one of the kids has said something unthinkable.

It is just me.

I stare at the sink, full of filth from the chaos of dinner that has just been.

I sigh.

Then I get up and do the damn dishes.

The main thing I can compare being a single parent with is the shock of bringing a newborn home, only to find yourself realising that no matter how many books you read, how many videos you watch, how much babysitting you did through high school, nothing can prepare you for the CONSTANTness of it.

There's always more to do. And you often don't feel like doing anything other than lying spread-eagle on the carpet while somebody empties your bladder and feeds you. Something. Anything. It is constant and unrelenting. You and you alone are responsible for managing the feeding, the washing, the comforting, the cooking, the listening, the cleaning, the driving, the scheduling, the tantrums, the talking back, the holy crap, the goddamn everything.

But what I haven't imagined is the loneliness. Once the kids are in bed, it is just me and the house. I can't leave to go out and I'm reluctant to invite over company lest I wake the kids. Well, that and the fact we're still only new to the area conspire to make my friendship circle shrink until it is more like a dot.

I spend the night-time hours when I should be writing, or reading, or doing something productive, frittering away online in the hope that social media may take the place of a social life. At least for now. And while my now ex-husband has leaped straight into the world of online dating (heck,

Chapter 7   The Year My Life Broke

I've even taken his dating profile pic and given him basic dating advice[7]) I am in no way ready for that.

I do the odd gig. One night the wonderful Dave O'Neil hires me to do a support spot in his comedy room. Headlining is Denise Scott, whom I absolutely love. I meet her just before the show and, as is common when meeting somebody you admire, try to walk the line between just connecting as human beings, and letting her know how much I love her stuff; and being really weird and makes it all feel uncomfortable.

It is a killer night; the audience is beautiful, Denise rocks it, I have a brilliant time, it is just one of those nights where you feel like 'YES! I love you, Comedy!' Afterwards I am chatting to Denise and say to her, 'You know, I was there that night when you won the Barry Award. And what I remember most is watching you and your partner dancing together and how he was just glowing with pride. My husband and I have just separated, it's so hard but no kidding, I often think of you guys that night and think: "Now THAT'S what I want."'

---

[7] For instance, I tell him to always smell good. Smell is a deal breaker for most women. And nope, Brut won't cut it.

Now for all I know, her perception of the awards night is different. Maybe he was completely drunk off his head that night, or just happened to LOVE the song that was on… I have no idea. But regardless, that moment has stuck with me. I want to feel THAT. To feel passionate and proud of each other. If I can't find that, then that's ok. I know that given the option of a lacklustre relationship, I'd rather just be alone.

Over the next few weeks, I slowly find a rhythm. My daughter, all twelve years of her, becomes my partner in crime; we are managing. The house is relatively – sufficiently – in order. The kids are fed. They are a little tearier than what was previously usual, but otherwise, we are going okay.

One night, I get a phone call.

'Jen? It's Ang.'

'Hey!' I say.

'It's Mum,' she says. 'She's really unwell.'

Chapter 7 The Year My Life Broke

'I know, I spoke to her today, she sounded a bit croaky but told me she's fine.'

'Well,' sighs my sister, 'she's not fine.'

The next morning, I say goodbye to my boys who are staying at home with Tim and catch a plane with my daughter up to Brisbane.

Our shuttle bus driver from the airport to the car rental pick-up asks what has brought us back, and I tell him.

'Oh,' he says softly. 'I looked after my mother in her final years, she passed away in 2011.' 'I'm sorry to hear that,' I say.

'The thing that you miss most is the advice. You want to ask them what they'd think of this and what they'd think of that. That's what you miss the most.'

'Wow,' I say, 'that makes sense.'

'Still, you know,' he continues, 'when she finally died, it sounds awful to say it, but it felt like a huge relief. Caring for somebody like that takes a big toll on you.'

'Mmmm,' I say, mentally discounting his advice. After all, I'm only planning to be here for a few days. It will take a week – at most – for Mum to bounce back…

When I arrive, Mum is lying in bed and is so cheerful that my first thought is that perhaps my sister has overreacted. She is as chatty and adorable as she has always been, and just so thrilled that we are here. Then she has to go to the bathroom. I pull back the sheet and see her leg is bright red and burning hot. She can barely move. This woman, this fiercely independent woman who insists on doing everything by herself, now needs each of us under an arm to help her into the bathroom some five metres away.

This is not good. This is not an overreaction.

Within an hour she is in hospital, never to return to her unit again.

Within days things are crystal clear. This is not going to be a trip of a few days. Mum is not going to be bouncing back, nor does she want to.

When her oncologist comes to visit, she says to Mum joking in the third person: 'So, what does Elaine want?'

Chapter 7 The Year My Life Broke

'Well sweetie,' says Mum, with a smile, not missing a beat, 'Elaine wants to leave this earth.'

'Well,' says the oncologist. 'I think that's completely reasonable.'

She is done. This is the final chapter. This is it.

So now what?

Mum is insistent that she is not staying in the hospital. 'I just want to be at home. Let me die at home!'

We try to explain to her that this just isn't an option.

They say that hearing is the last thing to go. But we know that for Mum, the last thing to go will be her stubbornness.

'Well then,' she says, 'just tell the doctors I'm moving in with Angie.'

To this day, I'm not convinced she didn't mean 'just tell them what they want to hear so I can go back home to my unit.'

But at any rate, my sister and I are desperately trying to get our heads above the water from our tears long enough to come up with solutions. We can't possibly move her in with Angie. Can we? No, hell no. Ang works full-time, her husband works full-time, and they have small children. It just can't happen.

A thought crosses my mind: should I move back to Queensland?

I broach it with my ex, who, almost to my relief, says 'HELL. NO.' We've just uprooted the family, both in terms of location and the basic structure of our family unit, now that we're separated. Another interstate move within six months IS NOT ON THE CARDS.

Right. That was that then. I would never dream of moving the kids away from him, so him putting his foot down means that I am absolved from the responsibility of making life a nightmare for everybody with another move.

That's that then.

So now what? I have to be there for Mum as best I can, that is unquestionable. But how to do it from interstate? Can I commute for as long as it takes?

Chapter 7 The Year My Life Broke

Our life becomes Groundhog Day. Ang, Ella and I spend the day at the hospital, drinking terrible coffee and eating terrible sandwiches (which Mum takes utter glee in saving, giving us as many of her meals as she can possibly sneak under her sheets, in spite of our protests. I suppose she feels this is the one bit of power she has. To feed us). We chat, we hug, we cry... then at night-time we head back to sleep in her unit, which now seems unbearably sad. On the third night after leaving hospital, I lie down in Mum's bed and sob so hard I begin to hyperventilate.

'I can't breathe!' I cry, panicked. 'I can't breathe!'

Ang and Ella lie next to me and rub my back and coach me to catch my breath again. Falling into the icy Toowoomba swimming pool in the middle of winter had nothing on this.

We have a billion things to organise. Paperwork. Packing. Decision making. But in that moment, Ang does something incredibly unproductive, yet perfect: she turns on the computer and hits play on a Jim Carrey movie and we laugh until we hurt. It is absurd to be laughing so hard – harder than we normally would, I think – when life is so shit. But my God it feels good. Thirty minutes in I feel like a new woman. It is like having a bottle of sparkling cool lemonade after trekking for days through a desert.

I love comedy and always have. I've spent the past decade being obsessed with it. But now with Mum so sick and all of my gigs in the foreseeable future being cancelled, things have come into a different focus. What the hell even matters? What makes a good life? Being onstage? Getting on TV? Having the fame and freedom to make whatever crazy projects I can imagine? Being able to do all of the above while raising kids? The kudos? Winning the love of strangers in an audience? Making people laugh? Following my passion and being able to make a living out of it?

Comedy suddenly seems so selfish. So me-me-me. So navel gazing and self-congratulatory and pointless. All about trying to come up with solid material that could get you the gigs that could get you the reputation that could get you the bigger gigs that could get you the money that could get you the representation that could get you the even bigger gigs that could get you the fame that could get you the guaranteed ticket sales that could get you the TV deal that could get you the fame that could get you God Knows What until it all falls apart one day and you are back to square one.

When there are people dying and families in distress and shit happening, what does comedy even matter? Does it at all? Even slightly?

Chapter 7 The Year My Life Broke

That night, watching 'Liar Liar', a mediocre mid-nineties comedy film, my sanity is saved. And it answers my question completely.

Comedy IS important. When this world is so full of pain, what is the response? Absence of any joy at all? Hell no.

Comedy matters. More than slightly.

> Comedy is pain relief.

It has served that purpose for me my entire life, and in the chapter that we are about to embark upon, it will prove to be one of our greatest life preservers.

Tim brings the boys up to Queensland during the school holidays so they can say goodbye. It is during this stay that he calls me to say that his family has convinced him it might be the best option to move back here, where he has more support.

And so... it is going to happen. We are all moving back.

It is fucking excruciating. I fly down to pack up. I finally understand the agony that ensues when you divide and disentangle an enmeshed life – for good. The physical evidence of our life together – the crockery and the kitchen appliances and the banal everyday shit we have accumulated – is easier to sort through than the hopes and dreams they represent.

The day it is all done and I start driving out of the Dandenongs – my beloved Enid Blyton dream life all but obliterated – I stop at my favourite bakery, buy a pack of lamingtons and in complete over-the-top-Jenny-style, put on Sia's track *Breathe Me*, which was the epically moving song in the final sequence of one of my favourite TV shows ever, *Six Feet Under*. (To this day, I maintain that these six minutes are the greatest ever ending to a TV series. Ever. Even if I just watch that few minutes alone on YouTube, I still cry like a baby struggling to latch onto a nipple. Just as Claire, the youngest of the family, drives away from her loved ones into an unknown future, leaving her past in the rear view mirror, so too do we drive away, further and further from this magical place that was meant to be our future but is now our painful past.) As I sing loudly to the music, with tears streaming down my face, I simultaneously stuff the lamingtons down my throat while spraying out flakes of coconut all over myself and the steering wheel with every sob, as the car becomes one very sad, musical snow globe.

Chapter 8 Life In The Departure Lounge

And so it is that 2014, which had begun so promisingly with a dream home and a dream life in the gorgeous foresty wonderland of the Dandenong's, has become me, a 35 year old newly-single woman, moving with her three kids and a dog into the basement of her sister's house in the suburbs of Brisbane.

#LivingTheDream

My kids are understandably devastated and displaced and out of sorts. I cannot blame them at all, nor can I offer enough emotional support given I'm already running on empty. I figure I can put their emotional needs on hold for a while, while I sort out the urgent nightmare of dealing with this logistical shitstorm, but if I'd had any idea how huge and long-term the effects of this traumatic upheaval would be on them; divorce, interstate moving, their mother grieving for and preoccupied with the imminent death of her own mum… well, I just don't know… but what else can I do? When the emotional needs of your dying mother are playing tug of war with those of your devastated kids, whose needs should come first? Who wins?

Mum is still adamant she is going to join us in this already insanely overcrowded set up.

We know it just isn't an option, so we set about finding others. Can we find a nursing home near Angie's house?

Which brings us to the adventures of navigating the world of aged care.

OH. MY. HEAVENS.

We are shocked to discover that almost every aged care option requires a sizeable deposit (most ask for literally hundreds of thousands of dollars), not an iota of which we actually have. They do of course, have rooms for people without money, but when I take a tour to see that kind of communal ward – full of many residents in a vegetative state – I feel like I am going to vomit. I walk in full of hope and optimism, resolute that whatever is available will just have to do; no matter how depressing it is, we'll just have to suck it up and make it work. But the reality of what that looks like makes me feel as though somebody has ripped out Mum's heart and punched me in the stomach with it.

Amazingly, we find a lovely private room, available for up to seven weeks a year for 'respite' care. Bingo. Realistically – and sadly – Mum won't be here in seven weeks, the place is lovely, and is ten minutes' drive from Angie's. Thank you aged care gods.

It is perfect. We bring her fish and chips, visit with the kids, read her books, watch movies, take her for walks around the garden. We couldn't have asked for more. Except that perhaps all this perfect joy is having an unexpected side effect: the seven-week deadline for the room is fast approaching and Mum doesn't appear to display any signs of going anywhere. I mean, she isn't bouncing out of bed and playing lawn bowls, clearly, but she isn't deteriorating nearly as quickly as we'd anticipated. That's the thing with death you see. Nobody really has any idea about the specifics of what will happen and when.

What are we going to do?

The only option is to move her upstairs into the communal ward. The residents there are in such a deteriorated state, both physically and mentally, that it's depressing the shit out of me. And I suspect that Mum will give up the will to keep going the moment she sets foot – or wheel, as the case may be – in there.

Is that the only option? Or is there another way? I broach the thought seriously for the first time: could **I** be her carer?

Ang and her hubby, Micko, say a resolute, and very practical, no. It would be too much. We can't bring her home. Ang books in to see the suite upstairs at the nursing home, filled with optimism that it can't really be that bad and we'll just have to make it work.

She returns home, mascara smudged under her eyes. 'Okay. Let's bring her home.' And so we do.

It is hard and beautiful and exhausting and wonderful and lonely.

And I am shocked by how incredible it feels. This work is undeniably helpful. Sure, I am hardly Mother Teresa looking after strangers I have no other connection to. This is my Mum, after all. But nonetheless, it feels like important

Chapter 8 Life In The Departure Lounge

work. Meaningful. It feels like I am putting my life to good use.

It certainly helps that I have the most grateful patient on the planet. 'You're so wonderful,' she says over and over again. 'I'm getting treated better than Prince William!' Given that she disturbingly says this while I am helping her on and off the toilet, I am not entirely sure where she's gotten her visions about the kind of care that the Royal Family receives.

Mum hates tattoos and makes no secret of letting me know she is not going to make an exception for me. She notices writing down my left forearm and says 'Oh gawd's strewth Jenny, what have you done to yourself now?'

I show her, explaining that it is her handwriting I've had tattooed onto me.

'Aww, be blowed!' she says, 'I'd never write on your arm!'

'No Mum,' I say, 'I took in a letter that you wrote me, and they copied part of it and then drew it on to me.'

She looks confused. Then understanding dawns. Then she seems genuinely touched.

We have this exact same conversation about six times over those last few months. Exactly the same. 'What have you done?' 'I'd never write on you!' 'Awwwww…'

As time drifts on and on, and Mum drifts in and out, I keep thinking about how I've spent my entire life trying so damn hard to make a mark, to create a legacy of work to leave behind so that if and when I am the one to suddenly depart this earth, I will at least be remembered.

But here is this woman who I love more than anything, who has not created a huge mark on the world that will be remembered by many. Does that mean that hers was not a good life? Of course not. It is shocking to me somehow to realise that when we die, we do not need to have created an impressive body of work to be remembered. We WILL be remembered by the people who love us. And I don't mean as in the 'I just LOVE Johnny Depp!' way, which is entirely dependent on a projection and can flip the moment bad behaviour hits the tabloids. I mean real love. The love of those who don't put you on a pedestal. Those who know you're good and bad. You're wonderful and awful. You're beautiful and ugly. They know all of that. And they would

Chapter 8   Life In The Departure Lounge

still give anything in the world to have one more moment with you.

One morning Mum sees me bawling my eyes out and cries out 'Jenny, my Jenny! Don't cry, I don't want you to cry!'

'It's okay Mum,' I say. 'It's okay. I know you have to go. It's just, I'm going to miss you is all.'

'I'm going to miss you too.'

I hug her and hold her hand. We chat for a while until her eyelids become too heavy.

'It's okay Mum. You go to sleep if you need to.'

'Okay,' she says. Then she opens her eyes briefly in wonder.

'Oh look!' she says. 'A flock of birds!' Then she falls into a coma.

For the next few days we bunk in with her, mattresses on the floor, so that she is never alone. We play Chopin – her favourite – and read her bush poetry and Rudyard Kipling. Even though it is inevitable it still seems so shocking that it is actually happening.

Ang and I join forces on the side of her bed one night and announce to her that we are going to perform 'our final concert for you, Mum!' and proceed to sing every war song we can remember.

In the middle of the night she suddenly begins moaning: 'Let me go, let me go.' Angie and I jump up to her sides and hold her hands. 'It's okay Mum, you can go. You can go.'

She grows agitated, angry even: 'I need to go! Oh, let me GO!' 'Mum, it's okay. You go.'

'LET ME GO!'

'Oh,' I say, thinking. 'Wait… do you mean… go to the toilet?'

She half nods.

'Oh! Okay Mum. Just go in your nappy.' Silence.

Then back to sleep.

Then Ang and I crack up laughing. Mum would have, too. God, we needed that.

Chapter 8   Life In The Departure Lounge

As the days chug along, my sister, who's been googling the symptoms of the trek towards the finish line, says to me, 'You know, I've read that at the end, right at the end, there can be a… um… a release.'

'Do you mean a number one or a number two?'

'I think it's both.'

I stare at her.

We know we're both thinking how much fun that will be to clean up afterwards.

'Well,' I say. 'Paper, scissors, rock?'

On the Tuesday morning, I approach her bed and announce loudly: 'Well Mum, I've had a wonderful shower, I've brushed my hair, I'm wearing clean clothes and quite frankly, I look amazing!'

I tell her that right now it's just me and Angie in the room, her girls.

I take out my computer and for the first time in weeks, I begin to write. The words just pour out; it's like a tidal wave of words about everything that's been happening have been backed up in the pipes of my fingers and just needed a chance to spill out.

I've literally written my final sentence of my barrage when Ang says 'Jen, listen. Mum's breathing has changed.' Anyone who's had a baby knows how you spend those last days counting down to your due date, looking for any sign of imminent labour, convincing yourself you can feel contractions, only when the real thing finally hits, you're like 'OOOOOOOH. THAT is real labour.'

It's the same with death. We've spent the countdown not leaving her bedside, checking her pulse over and over, looking to see if her knees were mottled, her feet cold, her colour changing.

Now, listening to her rattling breath, there is no doubt.

This is it.

We've had no word left unsaid between us, but what it comes down to at the end in her final moments is us both saying this. 'We love you, we love you, we love you. Thank you, thank you, thank you.'

And she is gone.

Chapter 9 Sometimes You Just Need A Nap

Weeks later, I finally pick up her ashes from the same memorial gardens where my mother had been laid to rest three decades earlier. The box is heavier than I expected (I guess when they say 'ashes to ashes' they don't factor in the hip replacements). I take her outside and stop at a chair under a beautiful tree. I sob and sob and sob. When I catch my breath, I jump in the car again and drive around to the spot where my real mother is buried. I grab the ashes out of the car and walk to my mother's gravestone. I sit there for the longest time. It is a stunning day. Cold, but the sunshine is beautiful and warm. It suddenly occurs to me to lay down and have a nap.

'No!' I think. 'I can't do that! This is a graveyard!'

Then another voice comes in. 'Of course you bloody can! It's your mother's plot. You can have a damn garden party here if you want to!'

On a crispy Spring day, I find myself napping in the sunshine on my mother's grave, her body metres below me, while I hold my other mother's ashes to my chest.

As if in a movie, I am suddenly hit by a montage of all the moments I'd shared in a bed with both of my respective mothers.

My original Mum warming my tiny freezing feet between her thighs in the mornings.

Me lying next to her, munching on almonds and reading my favourite book ever, 'Bruny and His Brothers.'

Bringing her a glass of water and squeezing in next to her on the mattress when she's sick, lying side by side and chatting, in what would be our final moments ever together.

Chapter 9   Sometimes You Just Need A Nap

Cuddling up to my second Mum with Ang and I either side of her, watching old movies and snacking on lollies.

Sneaking into her room in the middle of the night to watch Wimbledon, while she shrieks at the TV in horror at her favourite Boris Becker: 'Come on Borree! Stop lollypopping it to him!'

Sitting next to her as a teenager, with her gripping my hand more tightly and tightly as I confess to her that my first boyfriend and I have slept together.

Caring for her and holding her beautiful papery hands in her final weeks on this earth.

And finally, climbing onto the tiny bed with her after she'd died, Ang and I on either side of her, our arms curled around her tiny body while we cover her in tears.

The bed has always been a sacred maternal space.

And now here we are, in this quiet memorial garden, for the first time ever, all three of us, together. Resting.

Chapter 10 The Life Changing Magic Of ~~Tidying~~ Hooking Up

I t may not be the best timing to start dipping my toe into the dating world during such a vulnerable time, but I'm not exactly in a logically thinking state during this life chapter, and heaven knows, I need a distraction.

I actually – and probably foolishly – start putting the feelers out there while Mum is still alive. My profile practically writes itself: 'Single mother of three nursing her 90-year-old grandmother seeks understanding man to take me away from reality… hello fellas please form an orderly queue!'

Mum has told me with complete certainty that one day I will meet 'a treasure. And…' she says, 'when you meet him, you'll know right away.' I smile.

'But,' she adds, 'when you do meet him, you suss him out. Really suss him out, Jenny.' 'What do you mean?' I ask.

She ponders. 'Find out what time he wakes up, what time he goes to sleep and what he does in between.'

I don't do any actual 'dating' – given that my head really isn't in the right place – but I do really embrace the buzz of matches and bantering with strangers as an effective distraction from life. Or death, as it were. The thrill of it lifts my mood, even if it does seem a little absurd to be swiping right with one hand and administering morphine with the other. Besides which, it is a brilliant way to end a connection that I'm not digging: 'Well sorry, I have to go change the nappy of my 90-year-old grandmother now. Laterz… xxx'

In spite of my increasing use of the dating apps as a coping mechanism, I can't help but think that in reality, by inviting somebody into my life I would be introducing them to a horrible reality that nobody would ever opt into willingly.

'Who,' I ask Ang one night, 'would ever want to be with me when this is my life? **I** don't even want to deal with it.'

Chapter 10 The Life Changing Magic Of Tidying Hooking Up

Ang takes a breath and looks into my eyes. 'Somebody', she says simply, 'who loves you.'

After Mum has passed away, I finally tiptoe into the minefield that is meeting potential online matches in real life. The string of dates isn't so much disastrous as just 'meh.' People who sound great on paper – or on the screen – don't necessarily present the same way in person. Which is why when it comes to meeting up in real life with Jon, I am so nervous I think I am going to be physically sick.

He presents SO well, you see, light years ahead of the dozens of folks I've encountered thus far in the new world of Bumble, Tinder and e-Harmony.[8] He is insanely smart, eloquent and witty; he makes me laugh out loud in each and every online conversation we have. Already, I like him so much. As I walk down the pathway to the cafe to meet him, I am silently praying to the good lord David Bowie that this one will actually turn out to be who he seems to be. Added to this is the thought: 'He has three kids; I have three kids. Even if it DOES turn out that he's brilliant, would either of us actually be up for all that this relationship would entail?'

---

[8] Bumble, Tinder and e-Harmony are incidentally excellent names for guinea pigs. #PetHack #YouAreWelcome

GULP.

Spoiler: as I write this sentence, he's buttering toast in the kitchen and making me a cuppa. We've been together half a decade and we do indeed have six kids and a Labrador between us.

But back then, I have no idea whether it is in any way wise to be so excited, or if I am simply setting myself up for bitter disappointment and heartbreak.

On our first official date, we go to see… da da da DA… Bill Bailey!

Afterwards, we of course meet up with my gorgeous friend Hatty and venture backstage to catch up with Bill in his dressing room. Within moments of greeting him, JON MAKES BILL BAILEY LAUGH. (Cue music: 'I just died in your arms tonight…')

Later, as I am filling Hatty in on the horrifically gruelling year that was, I try to sum up where I am right now. 'So the next year is going to be a year of…'

Jon chips in: 'Rebuilding.'

Chapter 10 The Life Changing Magic Of Tidying Hooking Up

I swear I fall head over heels in love with him at that very moment, right in the dressing room of my favourite comedian who's ever walked the earth.

We then spend a good portion of our date watching 'bemused' as Bill and his crew play a game of bowling down the hallway – using stale falafels for bowling balls.

#BestFirstDateEver

#MagicHappens

Chapter 11 Episode IV: A New Hope

So now what? Moving back to Melbourne is unthinkable. simply cannot uproot the kids again, besides which, their Dad is now back in Queensland as well. My goal to be where the comedy is now feels like a distant broken pipedream, of which the 'pipe' part has well and truly burst. One day I see a teapot that says, 'Bloom where you are planted.' It seems that in spite of my best efforts to flee, *this* is where I am planted. Now how the hell do I begin to bloom?

I still love comedy, I do, but something has profoundly shifted in me. I can't just go back to the way things were. I want more. Was this going to be the turning point that changed everything and that shoved me into a new life where I found a beautiful and unexpected happy ending?

As they say, '#MagicHappens'.

But then again, as Tim Minchin says, '#SoDoesCotDeath'.

I have no idea what to do, or what any of this means, if anything. All I know is that in comparison to what I've spent these past months doing, comedy just feels so shallow. So 'Look at me! Love me! Give me attention!' I'd invested so much of myself in 'making it' over the years, but now, after finally emerging from the emotional cocoon that has wrapped me up for the past six months, in the words of Carrie Bradshaw, 'is comedy even a worthwhile pursuit?'

I love comedy for sure. But is 'doing what you love' really the ultimate pursuit in life as we're constantly told? I'm not sure. All I know is that I want to feel the sense of purpose that I felt while I was looking after my mother in the final chapter of her life.

Well what do you know?

Chapter 11 Episode IV: A New Hope

Through a stunning display of serendipity, I stumble across an audition notice for Clown Doctors.

Oh. My. Word.

I'd first seen a documentary about the Clown Doctors many, many moons ago and was blown away by the idea of going into such a heartbreaking environment to try to help provide comic relief to families' lives. I remember thinking at the time that I'd be way too sensitive for a job like this, however noble. I didn't think I could handle it. Yet I never thought I'd be able to cope with being a palliative carer either, yet that had been one of the – yes, excruciating – but also most fulfilling and beautiful parts of my life.

And so, I audition. It is an extensive and gruelling process – a group workshop day, then, once shortlisted, an observation round in the hospital to watch the working Clown Doctors and reflect on what I've seen and ask questions. Then finally, an audition out on the hospital floor working side by side with two different Clown Doctors on shift, followed finally by an interview which to my amusement and delight, allows me to tick off 'conduct a job interview wearing nothing but a onesie' off my bucket list.

I've never wanted a job so much in my life.

FUNNY MUMMY

The afternoon of my final audition, David Symons, the Humour Foundation's Artistic Director, calls me. I nervously but excitedly answer the phone and he tells me, 'We'd love to have you be our newest Clowntern.'

I scream so hard I'm surprised I haven't received legal papers to pay for his ongoing audiology expenses.

And so, that day, Doctor Jolly is born: Doctor Angelina Jolly.

Often when people find out that I do this, one of the first things they say is 'Oh my goodness, I could never do that, I'd get far too upset seeing the poor sick kids.'

And here's the thing: I was worried about exactly the same thing. I wondered how on earth anybody who has to deal with such sadness day in and day out is able to cope. Do you just distance yourself? Go into robot mode? Try to leave your emotions at the door? Was that how I'd 'coped' looking after Mum? And this is where the amazing part is: to do this job properly, to really be there for somebody, to bring the light into the room, you have to do exactly the opposite of shutting down. You have to show up with an open heart. Every day.

Chapter 11   Episode IV: A New Hope

Now that's not to say that doing so is easy. Many times it's really, really hard, but I remind myself that me being comfortable in that room is absolutely trumped by the need to be there for the child and the family. Shutting down your emotions means shutting down your connection.

I love this quote from the author Jonathan Safran Foer: "You cannot protect yourself from sadness without also protecting yourself from happiness." I believe this even extends further: you cannot protect yourself from pain without also protecting yourself from connection.

This rings true not just for Clown Doctoring, but for life.

I think sometimes about Shirley, that bus driver over in Las Vegas. I wonder if she's won the jackpot yet, or if she's still all these years later still waiting, still driving, still giving tourists advice on how to not pass out from the desert heat. And moreover, I wonder whether she is happy in the journey, in the waiting, and the hoping. I think about how pursuing a career in comedy is much the same; it's a gamble that may or may not pay off; it's a lottery.

Then I think, maybe it's not just comedy that's a lottery. Maybe life is. You choose the areas you want to put your tickets in – career, family, health… you increase your odds of success with the more effort you put in but, at the end of the day, unexpected shit just happens.

You can work your ass off, but your aspirations just don't align with the stars.

You can put everything into being a present, invested, solid parent yet one of your kids has a drug addiction.

You can eat well and exercise but suffer an aneurysm and die at 33.

So what? Does this mean you throw your hands up in the air, don't bother putting any tickets into any draw and just let things take their course?

I don't think so.

Because despite what we can't control, great things are still worth striving for.

I'm still a big dreamer. I still work towards huge creative goals, from writing and acting in a TV comedy, to speaking all over the world, to getting my PhD. I want to travel just about anywhere but with a special shout out to trekking

Chapter 11 Episode IV: A New Hope

Nepal. I want to live in Canada again. I want to perform around the world.

But somewhere along the line my focus has shifted from life being all about making these marvellous things come to fruition and life being *somewhat* about them. I'm not just spouting pastel bullshit at you when I say that nowadays I have regular moments – be they making pancakes for our bazillion kids on Sunday mornings, or curling up on the couch, scrawling in my notebook and looking across to my beautiful hubby, with a cup of tea in his hand and a very cuddly Labrador trying to snuggle on his lap, or going to an 80s dance class with my littlest and his cousins – it's here where I think that if this is as good as it ever gets, I am more than okay with that.

In fact, I will be stoked with that.

Chapter 12 What It's Like To Be A Mother In Comedy

I t's people – men and women alike – asking 'where are your kids?' when you're at work.

It's being overjoyed at being onstage when it's all you've dreamed of doing. It's being overwrought with exhaustion from late nights and early mornings.

It's being applauded for your efforts, then nose-diving back to a reality where you're not.

FUNNY MUMMY

It's going to work and thinking you're doing a great job, then coming home and thinking you're doing a shit one.

It's feeling guilty when you're missing the kids and feeling guilty when you're not.

It's taking comfort from your shittiest parenting moments knowing it's highly likely they'll become comedy gold.

It's boasting onstage about what a crappy mum you are, while secretly crumbling at the notion that it's true.

It's watching your peers without kids do all the festivals, all the touring and all the moving cities to grasp their careers with both hands, while you're scouring the house to find a coloured shirt for 'orange day'.

It's trying to tour with the kids, telling everyone it's an amazing family experience while battling a nervous and financial breakdown.

It's staying late at the festival club to schmooze and connect and be seen, while nervously fighting the urge to get a proper night's sleep for the kid-filled day ahead.

Chapter 12 What It's Like To Be A Mother In Comedy

It's leaving the house with the kids begging you not to leave, then walking onstage like you don't have a care in the world.

It's cracking up at your kids' utterings, then asking if you can use them in your set.

It's also, sometimes, **not** asking if you can use them. (Shhh)

It's looking at your family's finances and how your 'touring' and 'festival' shows have all but killed them, and realising that you may, in fact, have the showbiz equivalent of a gambling problem.

It's looking back at all the nights you weren't there because you were at a gig and thinking, 'I've fucked it all up.'

It's looking back at all the nights you didn't go to gigs and thinking, 'I've fucked it all up.'

It's coming home from a shitty, soul-crushing gig, then seeing your kids in their most beautiful state – sleeping – and smiling knowing that your worth is so much more than whatever you do onstage.

It's taking the risk that you'll develop a reputation as 'unreliable', when you have to cancel gigs when your kid is sick.

It's saying no. To your kids and to opportunities. Sometimes either of which you would die for.

It's knowing you're setting an amazing example as a role model for your kids in following their dreams, while questioning what kind of example you're setting as a parent.

It's reminding yourself of the truth that family is more important than any comedy achievement; but still glancing over the fence and hearing the whispers, 'But what if…? What if…?'

It's knowing full well that every struggle you're having is the struggle of every working mother everywhere.

And it's hoping against hope that every time you get onstage, these mothers after your own heart – your allies – are there somewhere in the audience. And that without words, you're raising your metaphorical glass and saying to each other:

I SEE YOU.

Chapter 13 Funny Mummies

I never expected parenting to be a walk in the park, but I never realised it would feel at times like a mad scramble through the apocalypse. Who the fuck am I? Where has the life I'd known gone? And what the hell is this unidentifiable shit all over the floor?

I say without hesitation what saves me from the darkness: being able to laugh.

Just two weeks before my second-born, Caleb, sprouts his head out, new neighbours move in next to our little rental cottage in the Brisbane 'burbs. Frankie is a relatively young mum like me, also preggers with her second, due any day. Her hubby is Norwegian and their little bundle of Scandinavian cuteness, Lilly, is two. Lilly promptly runs into our house and emerges minutes later with my daughter in tow, exclaiming 'Mama! This is Ella! She's MY BEST FRIEND!' Thus, it is decided.

If it were considered socially acceptable, I might well have done the same as Lilly. I do envy toddlers for being able to get away with that shit. But if I could have run into our neighbours' house and emerged with Frankie exclaiming 'Everybody! This is Frankie! She's MY BEST FRIEND!' I bloody well would have.

(Note to self: don't give up, make this happen someday.)

Now as anybody with a toddler and a baby will tell you, it is bloody, mind-numbingly, nuts. Not to get ahead of myself, but now as a mother of six in total, I can honestly say hand over heart that the hardest combo of ANY is having a baby and a toddler.

Oh dear heavens.

There we are, Frankie and me, both of us soon with our babies and a toddler each, slowly losing our minds, but doing so TOGETHER. It is magic. We share meals, bathe

Chapter 13   Funny Mummies

each other's kids and the best part of all: LOSE OUR SHIT LAUGHING. When the shit hits the fan – which may have quite literally happened, I don't know, I've blocked out so many baby poo incidents who can really say? – we find the funny in it and take turns trying to make each other's chest hurt from laughing too much. Of course, our chests already hurt. We are breastfeeding mothers. I didn't say the bar was high.

This is my first inkling that laughter and solidarity with a like-minded mama are keys to holding onto your sanity through the trials and tribulations of parenthood.

We put the kids to bed, then binge on fruit 'n' nut chocolate and *Sex and the City* episodes. We banter like banshees, we let it all hang out – hard NOT to do when you live next door and spend virtually every day together – about the shittest moments and feelings we are having, and we joke about it. She is the freaking best. And I'm confident that I can speak for both of us when I say that our friendship and ability to tickle each other's funny bones got us through the incredible stress of having small children.

One hot afternoon, we put an inflatable kids pool in Frankie's front yard for the girls, and they start playing with the hose. Inevitably we get sprayed, but egged on by each other, Frankie and I embrace it and soon take turns spraying each other with it and dancing around and hamming it up. At some point it strikes us that as breastfeeding mothers wearing now soaked-through clothes dancing for all in the neighbourhood to see, we look like some desperately sad incarnation of a suburban wet t-shirt competition.

We laugh so hard we quite possibly wee all over each other. We are already wet so who can say?

In 2010 the stars magically align, and we unbelievably manage to wrangle five days together, just the two of us, in New York City. We naturally take this opportunity to take a zillion photos of us eating chocolate in bathroom mirrors, in an art series we christen 'The Mirror Has Two Hershey Bars.' We decline to buy vibrators on the Sex and the City tour, in favour of smushing as many cupcakes as we can down our throats. We get our portraits sketched together in Times Square with a legendary result that still kills me with laughter every time I look at it. We meet Batman. We drink tequila at a bar called 'Wet Willies'. We climb into an unlocked police buggy while the security guard inside the police station sleeps (my skin crawls when I think of how much trouble we could have gotten into for that one!) We pose with the moon on Brooklyn Bridge. And we marvel at our much photographed hugely substantial but lopsided bosoms; as breastfeeding mothers away from home.

Chapter 13 Funny Mummies

Obviously, all of life cannot be a cabaret and all that jazz. But my God it helps if you're able to be a spoiled turd every now and then and have a fucking amazing jam packed experience so wondrous and intense and full of delicious joy nuggets that you can chomp on the memories of them in the far less spectacular of life's chapters.

Like I said, I used to think comedy was a luxury, but now I know it's a necessity. It's pain relief. It's connecting. It's breathing... with style.

Which brings me to Funny Mummies. It started as a passion project on Facebook, a group for mums to support mums by sharing laughter. To help each other chuckle, smile at the crap bits and to remind ourselves not to take this parenting gig so freaking seriously. We NEED this – the laughs and the sense of community – for our mental health, so that we can have fuller tanks with which to service all other areas of our lives.

Laughter and connection. That's what we need. The self-help parenting industry has been insanely damaging to mothers. Not to say there's not helpful information in there, absolutely there is, but the whole idea that's being promoted subconsciously to women – particularly via social media – is that you should be constantly striving to be the 'best you' you can possibly be and you know what?

I'm over it. It's why I created the web series 'How Me Parent Good: And You Can Too!'. It was damn hard work but so, so very cathartic!

I wanted to say through this series, 'You know what? The pursuit of perfection is exhausting. It's okay to fail. YOU WILL FAIL. Just fail graciously, smile, laugh it off and move on to the next thing.'

Besides which, even if you are the scientific miracle of the perfect parent, chances are you know how your kids will respond once you're all done and they're adults? 'Oh my GOD MUM! You were always so perfect, how the hell were we meant to live up to that?!'

It's okay to get it wrong. You're gonna. Because this gig is beyond constant. Raising kids is like having the world's worst roommates.

They pay no rent. They don't clean up after themselves, unless you're really lucky and/or you've put a shitload of effort into making it so, and even then, you have to check that they're actually doing it properly and in all likelihood you're paying them a small wage to do so. You cook for them, and not just any old shit, you really do think about their nutrition and urge them to eat the stuff that's going to be good for their health. They turn their noses up at what

Chapter 13 Funny Mummies

you make, insisting they don't like it and you either persist with it or give up and make them something else. You wipe their arse for them. You check on the quality of their stools, to make sure that their digestion is progressing well. When they're sick, you wait hand and foot on them and genuinely hurt with them when they're hurting.

You do everything in the fucking household and if you're LUCKY they will leave when they're 18 and and and… at the end of it? It's entirely likely that one day for your efforts, they'll present you with not a gold watch, not a bouquet of flowers, not a cheque covering the backlog of their rent owing but rather, the sentiment whether spoken explicitly or just harboured inside: 'You fucked me up.' Should this day come, I'm actually prepared.

'I fucked YOU up?' I'll say. 'I fucked YOU up? Listen champ, YOU fucked ME up! I used to have abs! I used to be sane! I USED TO BE A NICE PERSON GODDAMN IT! I NEVER EVEN USED TO YELL AND NOW LOOK WHAT YOU'VE REDUCED ME TO: TYPING ALL CAPS IN MY BLOODY MEMOIR WHICH IS MEANT TO BE CALMING AND POSITIVE!'

Anyhoooooo…

FUNNY MUMMY

My upbringing fucked me up. Their upbringing will fuck them up. Their kids' upbringing will fuck them up. It's all one massive babushka doll of fuckedupness but the thing is this: being fucked up by life doesn't mean you're defeated by it. It means you're coloured by it; moulded by it; shifted by it.

I'm trying to teach my kids this. To not be martyrs to the dark parts of their lives, which are inevitable, but to look for the meaning, to recognise it, to create it. I want them to read Josef Frankl's 'Man's Search for Meaning', to realise that even in the midst of the most unimaginable pain, that maybe one day, there will come a time when even the most awful experience may prove useful. That maybe it means you'll have genuine, deep empathy for somebody else who's suffering. That maybe you'll be able to offer counsel that you would otherwise never hope to possess. Maybe you'll create something, write something, offer something to the world that's born directly out of your experience, to share it so that others may find something in it that can help them.

Because after all my searching, all my questioning over whether comedy is useful or not, for wondering what actually does constitute a good life, I have come to one conclusion that I'm convinced is absolutely true: helping others is ALWAYS a good use of your life.

Chapter 13   Funny Mummies

This will look different for everyone. For some, it might be having a literally caring profession, whether that's being a nurse or physio or speech pathologist. For someone else, it might be that they put creative pursuits out into the world that touch people in some way, from music to macramé to

Irish dancing to sandcastles. (Just kidding. Nobody likes macramé.) For others, it might be taking on two little girls who've lost their Mum and raising them as their own.

In her final weeks here, I asked Mum what advice she'd want me to live by.

'Be yourself. Be happy,' she said.

'And make people laugh.'

Chapter 14 The Best Free Advice You Will Ever Get

(or 'What To Do When You Feel Like Shit')

Does this chapter title imply that I have the answers? Because, spoiler: I don't. But, as I said, this advice is free, so you're losing absolutely nothing by reading it. Well, except for the money you spent on this book in the first place. So, let's just pretend that the rest of the book was what you paid for and this bit's the free bonus. You're welcome.

I don't know much, but what I do know is this: **we need more laughter in the world.** And as the saying goes, or should go, at least – hilarity starts at home. With that, I asked my beautiful Funny Mummies Facebook group what makes them laugh, or what makes their happiest, particularly during times of extreme turd-ulence.

Here are some of their responses:

> *I listen to the 'My Dad Wrote A Porno' podcast, but not on public transport (too embarrassing) or while driving (I almost crashed the car once).*
> — Helen

> *Friends make me laugh. Singing makes me happy. And being barefoot in nature lifts my mood.*
> — Jacinta

> *Happy hour at my local pub makes me happy without fail.*
> — Ruth

> *Music, dancing, time outdoors, exercise, friends, a really great book and a warm cup of tea, chocolate and getting laid!*
> — Grace

Chapter 14 The Best Free Advice You Will Ever Get

Comedy! Live is best. There's something about being in a room with strangers, in the dark, in a non-sexy time way. Also, Officeworks. It's been proven impossible to be grumpy surrounded by rainbow coloured stationery products.
— Catherine

My partner giggling always makes me giggle too. He's got one of those laughs that when he finds something really funny, he has a hilarious laugh. Love those people.
— Ruth

My old school tunes really loud in my car going for long drives.
— Rajna

Happiest is when I finish writing a new song. Saddest is when I realise my band is still trying to find a singer, so we can actually start playing.
— Rebecca

I've discovered sound baths, particularly gong meditation. I feel amazing after a good gonging.
— Wendy

Dancing like a lunatic in the kitchen to old school 90's tunes. Feel like such a weirdo! Gotta love a good weirdo session! My kids looooove it when I

add the karaoke element to my session.
— Kellie

I watch Kitty Flanagan on YouTube – she never fails to make me laugh.
— Nicky

POO rhymes with the boys: 'If you're climbing up a ladder and you hear something splatter DIARRHOEA DIARRHOEA'. We have dozens of them, the imagination of boys is a fertile breeding ground when directed to toilet humour!
— Tracey

I sit in my car listening to Whitney on the decibels my ears can take while I munch down on an oversized block of chocolate singing each song like I am auditioning to the Voice.
— Radha

If I can't spend time with my grandies, I watch videos of them… especially the baby giggle ones. They never fail to put a smile on my dial. Oh… and goat videos – have any of you seen videos of baby goats in pyjamas???
— Lauren

This group *makes me happy! There's so much negativity and nastiness on social media. It's*

Chapter 14 The Best Free Advice You Will Ever Get

nice to hang out with ladies who are funny and kind to each other. It's my favourite place on Facebook.
— Kath

Dancing like nobody is watching. Especially when the kids are watching. And their friends are over.
— Amanda

A-freaking-men.

Smear your home, life and community with more funny.

Print out a Mister T poster from the internet and stick it on your wall giving directions to the toilet[9] and/or a poster of Lionel Richie asking if it's him you're looking for once you find said toilet.[10]

Be silly with your munchkins. Don't make the mistake of taking life crazy seriously, at least not all the time. I often find I can shock my kids out of a shitty mood by making them laugh. Sing, dance, do silly voices, be an evil mastermind chef while you're cooking dinner, whatever you gotta do, surprise yourself and the fam with your inner goofball. My hubby – who upon first impression is a rather

---

[9] We actually have done this.
[10] Yup, done this too.

refined and well-presented English gent – once cheered me out of a looming depression nose-dive by sticking a rubber glove on his head and feet, jumping onto the kitchen counter and clucking like a chicken. I kid you not.

Seek out comedy and make it part of your life. Bonus points for seeing it live, it's MAGIC, but find it anyway you can. Invite mates along to see shows with you and BAM! Laughter plus friend time. Two birds. One stone. All that.

However you do it, laughing out loud has got to be part of each and every day of your life. It's non-negotiable.

Make it happen.

Trust me.

I'm a (clown) doctor.

I am still trying to make people laugh. And I always will. Only now I know that it doesn't matter if that's on a stage in front of hundreds of people, in a hospital room in front of a family, online for people I'll likely never meet in person or with my family around the house.

Chapter 14   The Best Free Advice You Will Ever Get

Life is short
Laugh hard

Wow, now that really does sound like something you'd read on a boho cushion from Kmart.

Bonus Content

Want, no **NEED** to see photos of the journey described in these pages?! Follow this link to see the photo gallery and more:

https://www.jennywynter.com/funny-mummy-bonus

About the Author

'... a very funny, talented lady. I hope Brisbane realises what a treasure it has.'
— Steve Kaplan, USA Comedy Coach (has represented Jack Black, Nia Varadalos)

'Wynter is a smart and well-versed performer with a likeability that can't be taught... Jenny Wynter is, quite simply, wonderful.'
— Fringe Benefits

Jenny is an award-winning comedian, cabaret performer and writer who has performed throughout Australia, Canada and the USA.

Her awards include the ABC iView Pitch Perfect Award for her web series in development *Viking Mama*, Best Variety Show at United Solo Festival in New York City, Excellence in Cabaret at Melbourne Fringe Festival, a Green Room Award nomination for Best Cabaret Writing and the AusMumpreneur Big Idea Award.

Her debut comedy web series 'How Me Parent Good: And You Can Too!' won Best Conceptual Web Series at the Palm Springs International Comedy Festival and Best Web Series at the Worldwide Women Film Festival.

She is a passionate mental health advocate and founder of Funny Mummies, a group which aims to improve mothers' health through laughter.

She lives in Brisbane, Australia with her husband, three kids, three bonus kids and a Labrador called Bublé.

www.jennywynter.com
www.facebook.com/jennywynter
www.instagram.com/jenwynter
www.funnymummies.com

www.ingramcontent.com/pod-product-compliance
Lightning Source LLC
Chambersburg PA
CBHW071917290426
44110CB00013B/1386